GERMAN PHRASE-BOOK,

A GUIDE

TO

𝔗𝔥𝔢 𝔉𝔬𝔯𝔪𝔞𝔱𝔦𝔬𝔫 𝔬𝔣 𝔖𝔢𝔫𝔱𝔢𝔫𝔠𝔢𝔰 𝔣𝔬𝔯 ℭ𝔬𝔫𝔳𝔢𝔯𝔰𝔞𝔱𝔦𝔬𝔫 𝔞𝔫𝔡 ℭ𝔬𝔪𝔭𝔬𝔰𝔦𝔱𝔦𝔬𝔫;

FOR

THE USE OF STUDENTS AND TRAVELLERS.

BY

ADOLPHUS BERNAYS, Ph. Doc.

PROFESSOR OF THE GERMAN LANGUAGE AND LITERATURE
IN KING'S COLLEGE, LONDON, ETC.

LONDON:
JOHN W. PARKER AND SON, WEST STRAND.
M.DCCC.LII.

This scarce antiquarian book is included in our special *Legacy Reprint Series*. In the interest of creating a more extensive selection of rare historical book reprints, we have chosen to reproduce this title even though it may possibly have occasional imperfections such as missing and blurred pages, missing text, poor pictures, markings, dark backgrounds and other reproduction issues beyond our control. Because this work is culturally important, we have made it available as a part of our commitment to protecting, preserving and promoting the world's literature.

PREFACE.

The knowledge of a language consists in a knowledge of its words and phrases. This may be acquired in various ways; but each demands an exercise of attention and memory. If a person happens to reside in the country in which the language he wishes to learn is spoken, every one he hears may become his teacher, and the more he frequents the society of natives and converses with them the more rapid will be his progress. But if a language is to be learnt at home, books must be the chief instructors:—grammars, exercises, vocabularies, phrase-books, dialogues, literary works, every one in its way and degree will be of service, and should be perused and studied according to the opportunities and tastes of the student.

It is quite possible to learn a language correctly by mere conversation and reading. But the process, even when the learner resides in the country itself, is slower and more uncertain than when it is accompanied by a methodical investigation of the grammar, vocabulary, and phraseology of the language. Without such a guidance the student can never be quite sure, whether the sentences he hears or reads are grammatical, and whether his application of them is perfectly idiomatic.

It is to meet these difficulties that I have published the various works which are to guide the English student of the German language, and that I now add this new volume. It will show, in a graduated series of examples interspersed with numerous remarks and notes, how Germans express their thoughts in speaking and writing, and it is expected that the student will, by the combination of other words after the models and rules placed before him, endeavour to attain that familiarity with the idiom which alone leads

PREFACE.

to a satisfactory result. I could, of course, within the narrow limits I had to prescribe to myself, produce only a few specimens of every class of phrases, leaving it to the industrious learner to extend them from his reading. This is particularly the case in that section which exhibits in a few instances the various ways in which English verbs have to be rendered into German, as well as in the list of more peculiarly idiomatic phrases. The former, if they could effect nothing more, will teach him caution and close attention in the perusal of his dictionary; and the latter will lead him to note with care all the sentences he may meet with which, to be understood, must be freely translated, that is sentence for sentence, and not word for word. Similar difficulties exist in all languages, and arise from the comparative paucity of primitive words, which, in proportion as the mind and wants of a nation expand, have to be employed in derivative and figurative senses, an application which necessarily differs according to the genius of each people, and the foreign influences a language may have experienced in its progress.

I intend to complete the series of these small books by the publication of dialogues. They will not pretend to help a traveller to converse with an inn-keeper, a shoe-maker, or a tailor; since such conversations must always be at fault and cut short, if the stranger relying on them finds that his interlocutor does not happen to answer him as set down in the book. But they will be taken from the writings (chiefly dramatic) of the best modern authors and accompanied by free translations and notes, and will thus show the student how the most polished and best educated classes of Germany converse, and enable him, with the help of this Phrase-Book, to imitate their example and in time to converse with equal freedom and correctness.

April, 1852.

CONTENTS.

	PAGE
Substantives and verbs	1
Note on schreien	—
———— verdienen, Verdienst	2
———— Frau	—
———— sprühen and fliegen	—
Remarks on substantives (Rem. I to VI.)	3
Pronouns and verbs (affirmative, interrogative, negative and interrogative negative)	4
Omission of *to do* before infinitive and of *to be* before participles. (Rem. VII.)	5
Mode of address, Remark VIII, and examples in the imperative.	—
Use of the indefinite pron. es	—
Remark (IX.) on the same	6
The Accusative after verbs	—
One or *they* rendered by man (Remarks X.)	8
Nominative and Accus. differing (Rem. XI.)	—
Nominative and Accusative alike (Rem. XII.)	—
Note on pronouns and adjectives ending in el, en, er	—
Perf. and Pluperfect tenses (conj. of haben and seyn)	9
Active verbs, conjug. with haben.	10
Neut. verbs, conjugated with seyn	—
Future tenses (Remark XIV and examples)	11
Compound infinitives (Rem. XV.)	12
Verbs requiring the Nominative after them	—
Names of nations, and their adj. (Rem. XVI)	14
Formation of feminine appellations (Rem. XVII)	—

	PAGE
Examples of the genitive	15
———— of *to* rendered by the genitive	—
Genit. before the governing noun	—
Forms of the genitive (Remark XVIII)	17
Place of the genit. (Rem. XIX)	18
Compound substantives from the genitive (Rem. XX)	—
Examples of the dative	—
Forms ———— (Rem. XXI).	19
Use ———— (Rem. XXII).	20
Adverbial clauses, formed with in	—
Gender of names of countries etc. (Rem. XXIII)	—
Adverbial clauses with auf, an, zu, in and adverbs	21
Note on auf dem Lande etc.	—
———— hier, da and dort	—
Adverbial clauses with in, auf, nach, von, aus, and adverbs	22
Miscellaneous sentences on the foregoing sections	24
Note on steigen	—
———— stehen and stellen	—
———— bringen	—
———— Butterbrod	—
Supression of the preposition *of*	—
Note on putzen	25
———— lassen as expressive of cause	—
Note on the use of eben	27
———— manner of rendering-*servant*	—
Note on Hügel	30
Adjectives preceded by articles etc	31
Note on *any one*	—
Remarks on the declension of adj. (XXIV to XXVI)	33

CONTENTS.

	PAGE
Omission of ge in the past participle (Rem. XXVII).	33
Remark (XXVIII) and examples on separable compound verbs	—
Passive voice	35
Note on aus-, ein-, auf- and absteigen	—
Note on *but*	36
Remarks (XXIX and XXX) on the Passive	37
Remarks (XXXI to XXXIII) on the position of the nominat. and verb with regard to each other	—
Use of so after da, als, wenn (Rem. XXXIV)	37
Reflective verbs	37
Note on *advantage*	38
Remarks (XXXV and XXXVI) on the use of the reflective verbs	39
Manner of speaking to a person of his relatives (Rem. XXXVII)	—
Remark XXXVIII on the use of zu before infinitives	40
Substantives of time in the accus. (Rem. XXXIX)	—
Impersonal, or uni-personal verbs	—
Note on *much*	—
—— the position of articles	41
—— Mensch and Mann	—
—— the use of bald	—
Remarks (XL) on impers. verbs and their government	43
Note on fehlen, gebrechen, mangeln	—
Remarks (XLI to XLV) on impersonal verbs*	44
The conditional (examples and Remarks)	45
Form and use of of the subjunc (Rem. XLVII and XLVIII)	46

	PAGE
PREPOSITIONS.	
Of locality, without motion.	46
————, with motion	47
————, of rest and motion	—
Notes on *to lose*	48
—— *immer noch*	—
—— Saal, Zimmer etc. and entgegen	50
Es, used in the sense of somebody, something (Rem. XLIX)	52
Zu and in (Rem. L.)	—
Comp. words (Rem. LI and LII)	—
Which in the acc. never omitted (Rem. LIII)	—
Of rendered by von (Rem. LIV)	—
Prepositions of time	—
The Present employed for the Perfect, and use of the Perfect (Rem.)	53
Prepositions of origin, cause and consequence	—
Note on *since*	—
—— *last*	—
—— halber and halben	54
—— *order*	—
—— *bill*	—
—— *minister*	55
—— *print*	56
Abstract adjectives (Rem. LVI)	57
An, auf, her after substantives (Rem. LVII)	—
Place of some prepositions (Rem. LVIII and LIX)	58
Prepositions of connection	—
Mode of rendering *any* (Rem. LX)	59
Difference between klein Geld and kleines (LXI)	—
Note on *cousin*	—
Prepositions of instrumentality	60
———————— Restriction	—

---

* For possessive (in Rem. XLI) read passive.

CONTENTS.

	PAGE		PAGE
The Pres. used for the Fut. (LXII)	61	Subst. compounded with adject. (LXXIX)	73
Einzig used after ein and kein (LXIII)	—	Different manners of rendering verbs	—
Different prepositions explained (LXIV)	—	To be, rendered by seyn, es giebt etc.	—
Of rendered by Prepositions	62	Infinitive past rendered by infin. pres. after *to be*	78
Von, a substitute for the genitives (LXV)	65	*To be* rendered by werden	79
Zu representing both *of* and *to* (LXVI)	—	——, omitted	—
Substantives require the same prepositions as the verbs from which they are derived (LXVII)	—	——, variously rendered	80
		To be for etc.	—
Verbs implying a change require zu (LXVIII)	—	**TO HAVE.**	
Substantives taking no plur. after numbers (LXIX)	—	1) in the sense of "to hold"	82
Note on Part. present after *of*	—	2) with neuter verbs	—
Names of towns and countries undecl. (LXX)	66	3) in the sense of "to cause"	83
Remark on Scheu and Sucht (LXXI)	—	Notes on *gate, heap* and bei	—
Adverbial termination (LXXII)	—	haben 4) as "to wish" etc.	84
Of rendered by prepos. continued	—	—— in the sense of "to buy" etc.	85
Note on *work*	—	Idiomatic phrase of haben	86
—— bringen	68	To become, werden, geziemen etc.	—
To rendered by prepos.	—	To be able, können	87
Notes on *to meet* and *to put off*	69	—— like etc., mögen, können, dürfen	89
Notes on sprechen and *to think*	70	To be obliged, müssen, dürfen	92
—— gleich, sogleich, zugleich and on *thing*	71	Shall, should, ought etc. sollen	
Remark on *to be going, to be about* (LXXIII)	72	to will etc. wollen	93
		Miscellaneous sentences on können, mögen, etc. especially on the Perfect, Pluperfect, Future and Conditional	94
Remark on the use of von (LXXIV)	—	Note on *partner*	—
Rem. on the use of bei (LXXV)	—	Remarks on können, müssen etc.	97
—— *to* after "to send" (LXXVI)	—	—— the subjunctive	98
Rem. on the government of gehören (LXXVII)	—	To let, leave, cause, lassen	—
Rem. on *of* after subst. of size etc. (LXXVIII)	—	——, as Imperative	100
		Miscellaneous sentences on the foregoing verbs	—
		Remarks on *will* and *would*	103

CONTENTS.

	PAGE
To be called, etc. heißen	103
To see, to hear, to teach, to learn, to help	104
To amuse	105
— answer	—
Note on fragen	106
Remark on the prefix be	107
—— To apply	—
Rem. on "to like"	108
Examples on the same	—
To appoint, appointment, disappoint	—
to bear	109
Note on globe	—
Remark on participle after kommen, etc.	111
Being, participle and substantive	—
to bid	112
— bleed	—
— boil	—
— break	113
— call	114
— cure	116
Remarks on the Partic. present	117
—— half in relation to hour etc. etc. on the minutes	118
to carry	—
— change	120
— charge	121
— come	122
— disappoint	124
— dispose	125
— do	126
Rem. on zwar in a sentence	128
—— the omission of how	—
—— to do, to have, to be	—
to draw	129
Participles after prepositions	131
Note on Verhältnis	—
Peculiar uses of prepositions	132

	PAGE
Note on *neighbour*	133
—— *corn*	134
—— *prince*	155
Remarks on dieselbe, dieselben or solche, used for sie	138
Rem. on dessen, deren etc., used for the posses. pron.	—
Rem. he who, she who, etc.	—
—— wo used for daß, in welchem etc.	—
Rem. on *in* and *at* rendered by auf	—
Accessory clauses turned into adjectives	139
Note on Platz	—
Remark on the preceding mode of construction	140
Conjunctions	—
Remarks on *when*	142
—— da and so	—
—— *before*	—
—— the omission of als	143
—————— wenn and daß	—
—— *although*	—
Conjunctions (continued)	—
Remark on als and wie	145
—— *indeed*	—
—— *but*	—
—— *nor*	—
wohl, ja, doch, denn, schon, used as expletives	—
Remark on the same	146
List of the principal adverbs	147
Rem. on sach and fältig as terminations	152
Rem. on ordinal adverbs	—
Verbs expressed by more than one word	—
Examples of prepositions used adverbially	155
Miscellaneous sentences	156
Idiomatic phrases	162

GERMAN PHRASE-BOOK.

SUBSTANTIVES AND VERBS.

The father works der Vater arbeitet
the fathers work die Väter arbeiten
the mother sews die Mutter nähet
the mothers sew die Mütter nähen
the daughter knits die Tochter strickt
the daughters knit die Töchter stricken
the brother writes der Bruder schreibt
the brothers write die Brüder schreiben
the teacher teaches der Lehrer lehret
the teachers teach die Lehrer lehren
the pupil learns der Schüler lernt
the pupils learn die Schüler lernen
the beetle buzzes der Käfer schwirret
the beetles buzz die Käfer schwirren
the ass brays der Esel schreiet [1]
the asses bray die Esel schreien
the bird chirps der Vogel zirpt
the birds chirp die Vögel zirpen
the cloak covers der Mantel hüllet
the cloaks cover die Mäntel hüllen
the key locks der Schlüssel schließet
the keys lock die Schlüssel schließen
the girl smiles das Mädchen lächelt
the girls smile die Mädchen lächeln
the carriage rolls der Wagen rollt
the carriages roll die Wagen rollen
the broom sweeps der Besen kehret
the brooms sweep die Besen kehren
the little mouse squeaks das Mäuschen quicket
the little mice squeak die Mäuschen quicken
the horse neighs das Pferd wiehert
the horses neigh die Pferde wiehern
the pig grunts das Schwein grunzet
the pigs grunt die Schweine grunzen
the sheep bleats das Scha(a)f blöcket
the sheep bleat die Scha(a)fe blöcken

---

[1] Schreien means to cry or scream, and is applied to all kinds of crying for which the language has not supplied a special word.

SUBSTANTIVES AND VERBS.

the dog barks   der Hund bellet
the dogs bark   die Hunde bellen
the wolf howls   der Wolf heulet
the wolves howl   die Wölfe heulen
the physician heals   der Arzt heilet
the physicians heal   die Aerzte heilen
the brook is shallow   der Bach ist seicht
the brooks are shallow   die Bäche sind seicht
the river flows   der Fluß fließet
the rivers flow   die Flüsse fließen
the stream runs   der Strom strömet
the streams run   die Ströme strömen
the cock crows   der Hahn krähet
the cocks crow   die Hähne krähen
the son reads   der Sohn liest*
the sons read   die Söhne lesen
the man earns   der Mann verdienet[2]
the men earn   die Männer verdienen
the woman saves   das Weib[3] sparet
the women save   die Weiber sparen
the light burns   das Licht brennet
the lights burn   die Lichter brennen
the child calls   das Kind rufet
the children call   die Kinder rufen

the house stands   das Haus stehet
the houses stand   die Häuser stehen
the calf jumps   das Kalb springt
the calves jump   die Kälber springen
the fowl cackles   das Huhn gackelt
the fowls cackle   die Hühner gackeln

the eye sees   das Auge sieht†
the eyes see   die Augen sehen
the ear hears   das Ohr höret
the ears hear   die Ohren hören
the spark flies   der Funke sprühet[4]
the sparks fly   die Funken sprühen
the ox lows   der Ochse brüllet
the oxen low   die Ochsen brüllen
the boy plays   der Knabe spielt
the boys play   die Knaben spielen
the goat bleats   die Ziege meckert
the goats bleat   die Ziegen meckern
the cat mews   die Katze mauet
the cats mew   die Katzen mauen
the hyæna laughs   die Hyäne lacht
the hyænas laugh   die Hyänen lachen
the hen scrapes   die Henne scharret
the hens scrape   die Hennen scharren
the swallow twitters   die Schwalbe zwitschert

---

* From lesen, which is irregular.
[2] Also to deserve; as, der Verdienst is *the earning*, and das Verdienst *the merit*.
[3] Also die Frau, but which properly means *lady*.
† From sehen, which is irregular.
[4] Sprühen (related to the English spray) is only said of the flying of sparks. Otherwise to fly is fliegen.

SUBSTANTIVES AND VERBS.

the swallows twitter die Schwalben zwitschern
the lark warbles die Lerche trillert
the larks warble die Lerchen trillern
the dove coos die Taube gurret
the doves coo die Tauben gurren
the black-bird whistles die Amsel pfeift
the black-birds whistle die Amseln pfeifen
the sister draws die Schwester zeichnet
the sisters draw die Schwestern zeichnen
the ruby glitters der Rubin glänzet
the rubies glitter die Rubinen glänzen
the bear growls der Bär brummt
the bears growl die Bären brummen
the parrot chatters der Papagei plaudert
the parrots chatter die Papageien plaudern
the prince rules der Fürst regiert
the princes rule die Fürsten regieren
the philosopher thinks der Philosoph denkt
the philosophers think die Philosophen denken

I. All substantives neuter, and most masculine, ending in el, en or er add nothing to the plural.

II. Most substantives masculine of one syllable, and some feminine and neuter, especially those ending in niß as well as some polysyllabic nouns make their plural in e.

III. Most neuter and a few masculine substantives make their plur. in er.

IV. All of the last class, and many of the two former change in the plural the a, o, or u into ä, ö or ü.

V. Masculine substantives ending in e, some masculine and neuter in el or er, and all the feminine in e, el and er (except Mutter and Tochter) make it in n.

VI. All fem. derivatives (except those mentioned) and several masc., especially appellatives from the Greek and Latin, make it in en.

☞ *For detailed information see the author's grammar, especially the appendix.*

PRONOUNS AND VERBS
affirmative, interrogative, negative, and interrogative negative*

I see and hear ich sehe und höre
I eat and drink ich esse und trinke
I seek and find ich suche und finde
I learn and teach ich lerne und lehre
I tremble and smile ich zittre und lächle
it rains and snows es regnet und schneiet
it thunders and lightens es donnert und blitzt
it hails and freezes es hagelt und friert
we hear and they see wir hören und sie sehen
we eat and they drink wir essen und sie trinken
we seek and they find wir suchen und sie finden
we learn and they teach wir lernen und sie lehren
we tremble and they smile wir zittern und sie lächeln
I do not sleep ich schlafe nicht
I do not dream ich träume nicht
he does not notice er bemerkt nicht
she does not answer sie antwortet nicht
it does not rain es regnet nicht
we do not travel wir reisen nicht
they do not drive sie fahren nicht
do I reside? wohne ich?
does he write? schreibt er?
he is writing er schreibt
does she play? spielt sie?
does it thaw? thauet es?
it is thawing es thauet
do I not speak? rede ich nicht?
does he not send? schicket er nicht?
does she not joke? scherzet sie nicht?
do we not advise? rathen wir nicht?
do they not bleed? bluten sie nicht?
I taught, and he learnt ich lehrte und er lernte
I trembled and she smiled ich zitterte und sie lächelte
it rained and snowed es regnete und schneiete
it thundered and lightened es donnerte und blitzte
it hailed and thawed es hagelte und thauete
did we not teach? lehrten wir nicht?
did they learn? lernten sie?

---

* See *Word-book,* p. 14, or Gram. Rs. 122 to 125 inclusive.

did they not travel? reiseten sie nicht?
we did not send wir schickten nicht
I was not dreaming ich träumte nicht
were you not joking and laughing? scherzten und lachten Sie nicht?
we were bleeding, and they were trembling wir bluteten und sie zitterten
why were they smiling? warum lächelten sie?

VII. The verbs *to do* before infinitives, and *to be* before participles present are not translated; but the infinitives or participles are put in the same tense as the omitted auxiliary.

VIII. The third person plural is employed in speaking *to* one person or more, as well as in speaking *of* persons; except that when used for the former purpose the pronouns are written with capital initials. And as a foreigner speaking or writing German would hardly ever have occasion to employ the second person singular or plural, the third person is always given in this book instead of either.

IMPERATIVE.

come kommen Sie
go gehen Sie
see sehen Sie
hear hören Sie
bring bringen Sie
send schicken Sie
fetch holen Sie
write schreiben Sie
read lesen Sie

teach lehren Sie
learn lernen Sie.
do not travel reisen Sie nicht
do not work arbeiten Sie nicht
do not play spielen Sie nicht
do not eat essen Sie nicht
do not tremble zittern Sie nicht
do not smile lächeln Sie nicht
do not laugh lachen Sie nicht

USE OF THE INDEFINITE PRONOUN es.

who is here? wer ist hier?
it is a man es ist ein Mann
is it a woman or a child? ist es eine Frau oder ein Kind?
it is neither a woman, nor a child es ist weder eine Frau, noch ein Kind
are they women or children? sind es Frauen oder Kinder?

6 THE ACCUSATIVE AFTER VERBS.

no, they are men nein, es sind Männer
what was it? was war es?
it was a mouse or a rat es war eine Maus oder eine Ratte
it was not I, it was you ich war es nicht, Sie waren es
they were neither dogs, nor cats es waren weder Hunde, noch Katzen
where was it? wo war es?
neither here nor there weder hier noch dort
when was it? wann war es?
yesterday or to-day gestern oder heute
then or now damals oder jetzt
how was it? wie war es?
good or bad gut oder schlecht

IX. Es, as used in the foregoing sentences points indefinitely to persons or things, as to an object, and is therefore employed without regard to gender and number, while the verb agrees with the subject. It is the same with demonstrative and relative pronouns.

The Accusative after Verbs.

who loves the son? w-er liebt d-en Sohn?
whom does the father love? w-en liebt d-er Vater?
he loves the son er liebt d-en Sohn
which father loves his son welch-er Vater liebt sein-en Sohn
which son does his father love? welch-en Sohn liebt sein Vater?
he loves this son, not that er liebt dies-en Sohn, nicht jen-en
whom do you expect? w-en erwarten Sie?
I expect him ich erwarte ihn
whom do you mean, the brother or the cousin? w-en meinen Sie, d-en Bruder oder d-en Vetter?
I mean the latter ich meine d-en letzter-en
what are you looking for? wa suchen Sie?
I am looking for a stick ich such ein-en Stock
which stick are you looking for this one or that? welch-en Stock suchen Sie, dies-en oder jen-en?
neither this one, nor that weder dies-en, noch jen-en

have you a carriage here? haben Sie ein=en Wagen hier?

I have none ich habe kein=en

he had formerly a nephew, but he has lost him er hatte ehemals ein=en Neffe=n, aber er hat ihn verloren

she writes a long letter sie schreibt ein=en lang=en Brief

I know no one here ich kenne kei=n=en Mensch=en hier

people called him a philosopher man nannte ihn ein=en Philoso=ph=en

my uncle bought a live bear mein Oheim kaufte ein=en lebendig=en Bär=en

I have no great-coat; lend me yours ich habe kein=en Oberrock; leihen Sie mir Ihr=en (d=en Ihrig=en)

I do not see our friend, but I see his ich sehe nicht unser=en Freund, aber ich sehe sein=en (d=en sein=en)

do you see me? sehen Sie mich?

I neither see thee nor her ich sehe weder dich noch sie

I heard him speak ich hörte ihn sprechen

bring the book here bringen Sie das Buch her

lay it down here legen Sie es hier hin

leave the keys here lassen Sie die Schlüssel hier

I have left them below ich habe sie unten gelassen

what does your lady play was spielt Ihre Frau Gemahlinn

she plays the piano-forte sie spielt das Fortepiano

I have heard her play very often ich habe sie sehr oft spielen hören

she plays it very well sie spielt es sehr gut

what does that author now write? was schreibt jener Schriftsteller jetzt?

he writes a new work er schreibt ein neues Werk

I warm myself ich wärme mich

thou warmest thyself du wärmest dich

he washes himself er waschet sich

she raises herself sie erhebt sich

the weather is getting dark das Wetter trübt sich

we defend ourselves wir vertheidi=gen uns

you hold yourselves ready ihr hal=tet euch (Sie halten sich) bereit

they hold themselves ready sie halten sich bereit

X. *One* or *they*, relating indefinitely to a person or persons, are rendered by man which (like the French *on*) is used only in the nom. sing., the other cases being given by the possessive pronoun of the third person,

XI. Nominative and Accusative differing.

a) I ich — me mich we wir — us uns
thou du — thee dich you ihr — you euch
he er — him ihn who wer — whom wen
himself, herself, itself, oneself, themselves sich

b) Articles, adjectives (not preceded by a similarly declined word) and adjective pronouns take the same endings as er and ihn, wer and wen in the

Masculine singular.

the der	— den	which welcher	— welchen
one einer	— einen	none keiner	— keinen
each jeder	— jeden	many a one mancher	— manchen
other and(e)rer	— andern[5]	such solcher	— solchen
mine meiner	— meinen	ours uns(e)rer	— unsern
thine deiner	— deinen	yours eu(e)rer	— eueren
his or its seiner	— seinen	hers or theirs ihrer	— ihren

c) Ein a or an, kein no, mein my, dein thy, sein his or its, ihr her or their, unser our and euer your, which are always placed before substantives, are undeclined in the nominative but take en in the accusative.

d) Only those *substantives* are declined in the acc. (taking n or en) which take n or en in the gen. and dative also; those which make the gen. in s or es remain unaltered in the acc.

XII. Nominative and Accusative alike.

a) *Feminine singular, and plural of the three genders.*

She and her, they and them sie, the die; a, an or one eine; (no plur.)

---

[5] Pronouns and adjectives ending in el, er or en usually drop the e preceding these consonants when an e is added to them, and the two former take generally n instead of en.

none keine; which welche; each jede; many a one, or many manche; other or others andere; such solche; my or mine meine; our or ours uns(e)re; thy or thine deine; your or yours eu(e)re; her or hers, their or theirs ihre.

b) *Neuter singular.*

The das; one eines; it es; none keines; which welches; each jedes; many a one manches; other and(e)res; such solches; mine meines; ours uns(e)res; thine deines; yours eu(e)res; hers *or* theirs ihres.

Ein, kein, mein, dein, etc., before substantives, and in the sense of a, no, my, thy, etc., remain (as they also do in the nom. masc.) undeclined in both the nom. and acc. In consequence of this, adjectives, which may follow them, take the endings they want.

PERFECT AND PLUPERFECT TENSES.

XIII. These are formed, in active verbs with the present and imperfect of haben to have, and in neuter verbs with those of seyn to be.

a) *Conjugation of* haben.

Present.
ich habe I have
du hast thou hast
er hat he has
wir or sie haben we or they have
ihr habet you have

Imperfect.
ich or er hatte I or he had
du hattest thou hadst
wir or sie hatten we or they had
ihr hattet you had

b) *Conjugation of* seyn.

Present.
ich bin I am
du bist thou art
er ist he is
wir or sie sind we or they are
ihr seyd you are

Imperfect.
ich or er war I or he was
du warst thou wast
wir or sie waren we or they were
ihr waret you were

c) *Formation of Past Participle.*

Regular verb ge—et or t   Irregular (generally) ge—en

ACTIVE VERBS.

I have worked and she has played ich habe gearbeitet und sie hat gespielt

he has laughed and we have joked er hat gelacht und wir haben gescherzt

have the children not heard? haben die Kinder nicht gehört?

you have not heard the children Sie haben die Kinder nicht gehört

had you heard them? hatten Sie sie gehört?

I had sent it ich hatte es geschickt

he had bought a dog er hatte einen Hund gekauft

she had knitted a stocking sie hatte einen Strumpf gestrickt

we had had a good horse wir hatten ein gutes Pferd gehabt

had they felt the wind? hatten sie den Wind gefühlt?

it had rained and snowed es hatte geregnet und geschneiet

it had thundered and lightened es hatte gedonnert und geblitzt

Observe that participles and infinitives are always placed at the end of the sentence.

NEUTER VERBS.

Irregular Participles.

been gewesen
become geworden
come gekommen
gone gegangen

run gelaufen
grown gewachsen
recovered genesen
happened geschehen

I have been an actor ich bin ein Schauspieler gewesen

she has also been an actress sie ist auch eine Schauspielerinn gewesen

he has been a tailor and his *daughter has* become a milliner

er ist ein Schneider gewesen und seine Tochter ist eine Putzmacherinn geworden

we have been watchmakers wir sind Uhrmacher gewesen

they have become shoe-makers sie sind Schuhmacher geworden

FUTURE TENSES.

what have you been? was sind Sie gewesen?
he has come alone er ist allein gekommen
they have gone together sie sind zusammen gegangen
have the trees not grown? sind die Bäume nicht gewachsen?
I had become ill, but had soon recovered ich war krank geworden, aber war bald genesen
had she not run fast? war sie nicht schnell gelaufen?

one had come einer war gekommen
none had gone there keiner war hingegangen
we had been soldiers wir waren Soldaten gewesen
they had become officers sie waren Officiere geworden
had you not recovered? waren Sie nicht genesen?
what had happened? was war geschehen?

FUTURE TENSES.

XIV. Formed by means of the present tense of werden to become, viz.:—

ich werde I become
du wirst thou becomest
er wird he becomes

wir or sie werden we or they become
ihr werdet you become

I shall be his friend ich werde sein Freund seyn
he will become his enemy er wird sein Feind werden
she will become his enemy sie wird seine Feindinn werden
she will have a letter sie wird einen Brief haben

I shall have been his friend ich werde sein Freund gewesen seyn

we shall send an answer wir werden eine Antwort schicken
we shall send, if you come wir werden schicken, wenn Sie kommen
they will come, if you send sie werden kommen, wenn Sie schicken
shall you not ride or drive? werden Sie nicht reiten oder fahren?

he will have become your enemy er wird Ihr Feind geworden seyn she will have had a long letter ſie wird einen langen Brief gehabt haben

we shall have sent a favorable answer wir werden eine günſtige Antwort geſchickt haben

they will have sent, before you come ſie werden geſchickt haben, ehe Sie kommen

they will have come, before you send ſie werden gekommen ſeyn, ehe Sie ſchicken

I shall have ridden too long ich werde zu lange geritten haben

she will have driven too fast ſie wird zu ſchnell gefahren ſeyn

XV. In the compound infinitive we employ the infinitive of the same auxiliary with which a verb would conjugate its perfect and pluperfect tenses, and always place it *after* the past participle.

To Be, To Become, and other Verbs which require the Nominative after them.

What are you? was ſind Sie?

I am an Englishman ich bin ein Engländer

what is she? was iſt ſie?

she is an English woman ſie iſt eine Engländerinn

we are Englishmen and they are Germans wir ſind Engländer und ſie ſind Deutſche

what was he? was war er?

he was a Frenchman er war ein Franzoſe

we were Frenchmen wir waren Franzoſen

they were Swedes ſie waren Schweden

were you also a Swede? waren Sie auch ein Schwede?

no, I was a Dane nein, ich war ein Däne

I am becoming an Austrian ich werde ein Oeſt(er)reicher

they are also becoming Austrians ſie werden auch Oeſt(er)reicher

he is becoming an Italian and sh is becoming a Spaniard er wird ein Italiener und ſie wird eine Spanierinn

we become Scotchmen and you become Irishmen wir werden Schotten und Sie werden Irländer

I became a Prussian and she became an Irish woman ich wurde ein Preuße und sie wurde eine Irländerinn

we became Prussians and they became Bavarians wir wurden Preußen und sie wurden Baiern

do you not seem an Arab? scheinen Sie nicht ein Araber?

do not become a Mohammedan werden Sie nicht ein Mahomebaner

I have been a Swiss ich bin ein Schweizer gewesen

he has been a Milanese and she has been a Venetian er ist ein Mailänder gewesen und sie ist eine Venetianerinn gewesen

we have been Hanoverians wir sind Hannoveraner gewesen

these women have been Hanoverians diese Weiber sind Hannoveranerinnen gewesen

what have you been? was sind Sie gewesen?

he has become a Genevese er ist ein Genfer geworden

they will become Genevese sie werden Genfer werden

I had been a Saxon ich war ein Sachse gewesen

she had become a Hessian sie war eine Hessinn geworden

they had become Hungarians sie waren Ungarn geworden

had you not become a Bohemian? waren Sie nicht ein Böhme geworden?

I shall become a European ich werde ein Europäer werden

he will become an Asiatic er wird ein Aster (or Asiate) werden

he will be an African er wird ein Afrikaner seyn

we shall be Americans wir werden Amerikaner seyn

they will become Dutchmen sie werden Holländer werden

he seems a Tyrolese er scheint ein Tyroler

they seemed to be Venetians sie schienen Venetianer zu seyn

he had seemed a Chinese er hatte ein Chinese geschienen

you are a Russian; remain one Sie sind ein Russe; bleiben Sie einer

she has always remained a Turkish woman sie ist immer eine Türkinn geblieben

he will remain a Portuguese er wird ein Portuglese bleiben

what is this man's name? wie heißt dieser Mann?
his name is John er heißt Johannes
what is your name? wie heißen Sie?
my name is Adolphus ich heiße Adolf
what is the name of this town? wie heißt diese Stadt?
it is called Venice sie heißt Venedig
what are these hills called? wie heißen diese Berge?
they are called the Vosges mountains sie heißen die Vogesen

he is called a Russian, but he is a Pole er heißt ein Russe, aber er ist ein Pole
what is the name of this tree in German? wie heißt dieser Baum auf Deutsch?
what is this called in English? wie heißt dieses auf Englisch?
this stone is called in French *pierre-de-taille*, in German *Quaderstein*, in English free-stone dieser Stein heißt auf Französisch *pierre-de-taille*, auf Deutsch Quaderstein und auf Englisch *free-stone*.

XVI. There are in German names for the inhabitants of most countries besides adjectives referring to the same. Thus:

Englishman Engländer — English englisch
Scotchman Schottländer — Scotch schottisch
Irishman Irländer — Irish irisch
Italian Italiener — Italian italienisch
Frenchman Franzose — French französisch
Turk Türke — Turkish türkisch

the French are lively die Franzosen sind lebhaft
this is French silk dies ist französische Seide

I learn French, or the French language ich lerne Französisch, oder die französische Sprache

XVII. Feminine appellations are generally made by the addition of the syllable inn (or in) and changing the vowel a, o or u of the *root into ä, ö, ü.*

The Genitive.

the buzzing of the beetle	das Schwirren d=es Käfer=s
the buzzing of the beetles	das Schwirren d=er Käfer
the braying of the ass	das Geschrei d=es Esel=s
the instruction of the teacher	der Unterricht d=es Lehrer=s
the labour of the father	die Arbeit d=es Vater=s
the education of the mother	die Erziehung d=er Mutter
the song of (the) birds	der Gesang d=er Vögel
the neighing of the horse	das Wiehern d=es Pferd=es
the howling of the wolf	das Geheul d=es Wolf=es
the barking of my dog	das Gebell mein=es Hund=es
the crowing of their cock	das Krähen ihr=es Hahn=es
the earning of that man	der Verdienst jen=es Mann=es
the economy of this woman	die Sparsamkeit dies=es Weib=es
the flying of a spark	das Sprühen ein=es Funke=ns
the play of his boy	das Spielen sein=es Knabe=n
the growling of a bear	das Gebrumm ein=es Bär=en
the reign of that prince	die Regierung jen=es Fürst=en

To rendered by the Genitive.

secretary to the minister Secretär d=es Minister=s	valet to the governor Kammerdiener d=es Gouverneur=s (Statthalter=s)
cook of the post-master Koch (Köchinn) d=es Postmeister=s	maid to his lady Kammerjungfer sein=er Gemahlinn

Genitive before the governing noun.

the cloak of the brother, or the brother's cloak der Mantel d=es Bruder=s, oder d=es Bruder=s Mantel

the handle of the knife, or the knife's handle der Stiel d=es Messer=s, oder d=es Messer=s Stiel

the hilt of the sword, or the sword's hilt der Griff d=es Degen=s, oder d=es Degen=s Griff

the handle of the chest, or the chest's handle die Handhabe d=es Kasten=s, oder d=es Kasten=s Handhabe the aunt of my cousin, or my cousin's aunt die Tante mein=es Vetter=s, oder meine=s Vetter=s Tante

the height of the mountain-range, or the range's height die Höhe d=es Gebirge=s, oder d=es Gebirge=s Höhe

the duty of this son, or this son's duty die Pflicht dies=es Sohn=(e)s, oder dies=es Sohn=(e)s Pflicht

the conduct of that child, or that child's conduct das Benehmen jen=es Kind=es, oder jen=es Kin= d=es Benehmen

the value of your money, or your money's value der Werth Ihr=es Geld=es, oder Ihr=es Geld=es Werth

the power of the storm, or the storm's power die Gewalt d=es Sturm=(e)s, oder d=es Sturm=(e)s Gewalt

the influence of Christianity, or Christianity's influence der Ein= fluß d=es Christenthum=(e)s, oder d=es Christenthum=(e)s Einfluß

the universality of our faith. or our faith's universality die Allge= meinheit unser=s Glaube=ns, oder *unser=s Glaube=ns Allgemeinheit*

the swiftness of no thought, or no thought's swiftness die Schnel= ligkeit kein=es Gedanke=ns, oder kein=es Gedanke=ns Schnelligkeit

the vivacity of his boy, or his boy's vivacity die Lebhaftigkeit sein=es Knabe=n, oder sein=es Knabe=n Lebhaftigkeit

the strength of the lion, or the lion's strength die Stärke d=es Löwe=n, oder d=es Löwe=n Stärke

the subjects of the prince, or the prince's subjects die Unterthan=en d=es Fürst=en, oder d=es Fürst=en Unterthan=en

the life of man, or man's life das Leben d=es Mensch=en, oder d=es Mensch=en Leben

the doctrine of every philosopher, or every philosopher's doctrine die Lehre jed=es Philosoph=en, oder jed=es Philosoph=en Lehre

the affection of a mother, or a mother's affection die Liebe ein=er Mutter, oder ein=er Mutter Liebe

the condescension of the queen, or the queen's condescension die Herablassung d=er Königinn, oder d=er Königinn Herablassung

the cloaks of the brothers, or the brother's cloaks die Mäntel d=er Brüder, oder d=er Brüder Mäntel the friendship of such a daughter, or such a daughter's friendship die Freundschaft ein=er solchen Tochter, oder ein=er solchen Tochter Freundschaft

the handles of the knives, or the knives' handles die Stiel=e d=er Messer, oder d=er Messer Stiel=e

the duties of these sons, or these sons' duties die Pflicht=en dies=er Söhn=e, oder dies=er Söhn=e Pflicht=en

the conduct of those children, or those children's conduct das Benehmen jen=er Kind=er, oder jen=er Kind=er Benehmen

the influences of riches, or riches' influences die Einflüss=e d=er Reichthüme=r, oder d=er Reichthüm=er Einflüss=e

the games of such boys, or such boys' games die Spiel=e solch=er Knabe=n, oder solch=er Knabe=n Spiel=e

the doctrines of all philosophers, or all philosophers' doctrines die Lehre=n all=er Philosoph=en, oder all=er Philosoph=en Lehre=n

the friendship of such daughters, or such daughters' friendship die Freundschaft solch=er Töchter, oder solch=er Töchter Freundschaft

XVIII. *Forms of the Genitive.*

a) of me   meiner   of us   unser
     of thee   deiner   of you   euer
     of him or of it   seiner   of her or of them   ihrer
     whose (interrogative) wessen

	Masc. and Neut.	Femin. and Plur. of 3 genders.
b) of the	d=es	d=er
of a or one	ein=es	ein=er
of this (these)	dies=es	dies=er
of that (those)	jen=es	jen=er
of which	welch=es	welch=er
whose (relat.)	dess=en	deren (or derer)
of my or mine	mein=es	mein=er
of thy or thine	dein=es	dein=er, etc.

c

THE GENITIVE.

All articles, adjective pronouns, and adjectives taking in the masc. and neut. es, and in the fem. and plur. er.

c) *Substantives* of the neuter, and by far the greater number of the *masc.* gender form their Gen. sing. in s or es, and in a few instances in ns; the masc. which do not so, take n or en. *Feminine* substantives remain unaltered in the sing. And in the plural ALL subst. are in the gen. as in the nom. and acc.

XIX. The genitive may, as in English, be placed before the governing noun, which then always drops the article by which it would be preceded, if it stood before the gen. Substantives taken in a general sense, as in the expression, *the life of man*, take the def. art. in German, especially in the sing., and in the gen., dat., and acc., and when they are not preceded by an adjective.

XX. The genitive before the governing subst. is often joined to it so as to make a compound word, the last determining both the gender and declension. Yet the manner of connecting them cannot be easily defined.

die Mutterliebe maternal love
die Kindespflicht filial duty
die Sohnespflicht the duty of a son
die Sohnespflichten the duties of a son
der Friedenstörer disturber of peace
der Menschenfreund philanthropist
der Weltbürger citizen of the world
die Sonnenfinsterniß eclipse of the sun
die Mond(s)finsterniß eclipse of the moon

das Erdbeben earth-quake
der Kanonendonner thunder (roar) of cannons
die Hautkrankheiten diseases of the skin
die Menschenkenntniß knowledge of men
das Vaterhaus paternal house
der Hausvater father of a family
die Knabenspiele sports of boys
die Mannesstärke manly strength
die Fürstenehre honour of princes

The Dative.

he gave his neighbour a light er *gab sein=em Nachbar ein Licht*

they made the father a present sie machten d=em Vater ein Geschenk

THE DATIVE.

go and fetch me the wine gehen Sie und holen Sie mir den Wein

have you fetched your brother his papers? haben Sie Ihr=em Bru=der seine Papiere geholt?

she hemmed the boy his handkerchiefs sie säumte d=em Kna=be=n seine Taschentücher

why do you not facilitate the man's labour? warum erleichtern Sie nicht dem Mann=(e) die Ar=beit?

he related the story to his son and daughter, in short to all his children er erzählte die Ge=schichte sein=em Sohn=(e) und sein=er Tochter, kurz all=en sein=en Kind=ern

repeat to me all wiederholen Sie mir Alles

I told it to my friends ich sagte es mein=en Freund=en

the thieves have stolen his money die Diebe haben ihm sein Geld gestohlen

they also took from him his clothes and linen sie nahmen ihm auch seine Kleider und (seine) Wäsche

they left him nothing sie ließen ihm nichts

I am much obliged to your cousin ich bin Ihr=em Vetter sehr ver=bunden

this hat is too large for the child dieser Hut ist dem Kind=(e) zu groß

XXI. *Forms of the Dative.*

a) to me mir
    to thee dir
    to him, to it ihm

to us uns
to you euch (or Ihnen)
to her ihr to them ihnen

	Masc. and Neut.	Fem.	Plur.
b) to the	d=em	d=er	d=en
to a	ein=em	ein=er	(none)
to this	dies=em	dies=er	dies=en
to that	jen=em	jen=er	jen=en
to which	welch=em	welch=er	welch=en
to all	all=em	all=er	all=en

and so on, the masc. and neut. taking em, the fem. er, and the plur. of three genders en.

XXII. The dative is used *to* express, not only the person (or thing) for whose benefit an action is performed; but also one which suffers a loss by it; also instead of *for* connected with *to*, and with many verbs which in English seem to govern the acc. or are followed by a preposition.

ADVERBIAL CLAUSES OF LOCALITY, ANSWERING TO THE QUESTIONS WHERE, WHEREIN, WHEREON, &C., EXPRESSED BY PREPOSITIONS GOVERNING THE DATIVE.

a) IN *rendered by* in.

in the house in dem Hause
in the room in dem Zimmer
in the drawing-room in dem Saale
in the bed-room in dem Schlafzimmer
in the dining-room in dem Speisesaale
in the garden in dem Garten
in the yard in dem Hofe
in the stables in dem Stalle
in town in der Stadt
in the (or at) church in der Kirche
in the kitchen in der Küche
in the cellar in dem Keller
in the (or at) school in der Schule
in the theatre in dem Theater (Schauspiel)

in the concert in dem Concert
in England in England
in Germany in Deutschland
in Scotland in Schottland
in Ireland in Irland
in France in Frankreich
in Italy in Italien
in Rome in Rom
in Milan in Mailand
in Austria in Oestreich
in Prussia in Preußen
in Russia in Rußland
in Sweden in Schweden
in Denmark in Dänemark
in Turkey in der Türkei
in Switzerland in der Schweiz
abroad im Auslande

XXIII. The great majority of names of countries, provinces, towns etc. are neut., and never take an article before them, unless they are preceded by an adjective. A few of the first named are, however, feminine, and these are always preceded by the def. article.

ADVERBIAL CLAUSES OF LOCALITY.

b) In *or* At *rendered by* auf.

in the street auf der Straße	in the town-house auf dem Stabt-hause
in (or at) the market auf dem Markte	
in the fencing-room auf dem Fechtboden [saale	at the university, or at College auf der Universität
in the ball-room auf dem Tanz-	in the country auf dem Lande
at the ball auf dem Balle	in the field auf dem Felde[6]

c) On, *rendered by* auf *or* an; *also on or by*, *by* zu.

on change auf der Börse	on leave auf Urlaub
on the continent auf dem Continente (Festlande)	on foot zu Fuße
	on horse-back zu Pferde
on board an Bord (auf dem Schiffe)	by a carriage zu Wagen
on the roof auf dem Dache	by water zu Wasser
on the hills auf dem Gebirge	by land zu Lande
on earth auf Erden	by sea zur See
on credit auf Borg (or Credit)	

d) In *or* At *rendered by* zu *or* in.

at home zu Hause	in or at Frankfort zu (in) Frankfurt
in London zu (in) London	in or at Warsaw zu (in) Warschau

Adverbs of place, used with verbs not expressing motion.

within drinnen — without draußen	on this side dießseits (hüben)
above oben, droben	on that side jenseits (drüben)
below unten, drunten	here hier, da[7]
behind hinten	there dort, da
before vorn	

---

[6] In dem Lande means, not abroad. (dans le pays), and in dem Felde is used only in relation to an army.

[7] Da is used for here when only one place is pointed out. When two are mentioned, we may say hier and da or hier and dort.

ADVERBIAL CLAUSES ANSWERING TO WHERETO, ETC. EXPRESSED BY PREPOS. GOVERNING THE ACCUS. OR DAT.

a) INTO (*or* TO *in the sense of into*) *rendered by* in *with the accusative.*

into the house in das Haus
into the room in das Zimmer
into the drawing-room in den Saal
into the yard in den Hof
into the school in die Schule

to church in die Kirche
to the play in's Theater
to Switzerland in die Schweiz
to Turkey in die Türkei
into the stables in den Stall

b) INTO *or* TO *rendered by* auf *with the accusative.*

into the street auf die Straße
to the market auf den Markt
and so on, as above

to the town-house auf's Rathhaus

c) TO *with verbs of motions directed to persons, by* zu, *with the dative.*

to whom will he go? zu wem wird er gehen?

to the father zu dem Vater
to the mother zu der Mutter

to the fathers and to the mothers zu den Vätern und zu den Müttern

to the daughters and to the sons zu den Töchtern und zu den Söhnen

to the man and to the woman zu dem Manne und zu dem Weibe

to the men and to the women

zu den Männern und zu den Weibern

to the boy and to the sister zu dem Knaben und zu der Schwester

to the boys and to the sisters zu den Knaben und zu den Schwestern

to the prince and to the colonel zu dem Fürsten und zu dem Obristen

to the princes and to the colonels zu den Fürsten und zu den Obristen *d)* To *with verbs of motion, directed to places, by* nach *with the dative.*

where does he go to? wohin geht er? or wo geht er hin?
home nach Hause
to that place nach jenem Orte
to Cologne nach Köln
to Aix-la-chapelle nach Aachen
to Liege nach Lüttich
to Poland nach Polen
to India nach Indien
to Franconia nach Franken
to Styria nach der Steiermark
to the Palatinate nach der Pfalz
to Crimea nach der Krimm
to Africa, Asia and America nach Afrika, Asien und Amerika
to Lusatia nach der Lausitz

e) From, von *or* aus *with the dative.*

whence does he come, or where does he come from? woher kömmt er? or wo kömmt er her?
from the house or garden aus dem Hause oder Garten
from the counting-house aus dem Comptoir or aus der Schreibstube
from home von Hause
from court vom Hofe
from the continent vom Continent
from the high-road von der Landstraße
from the Hague or from Nimuegen vom Haag* oder von Nimwegen
from the Moldavia and Walachia von der Moldau und Walachei

Adverbs of Locality, expressive of Motion.

whither? wohin?

Towards the speaker:
hither her
in herein
out heraus
up herauf
down { herab / herunter
over herüber
to and fro hin und her
up and down (backwards and forwards) auf und ab

From the speaker:
hither hin
hinein
hinaus
hinauf
hinab
hinunter
hinüber

---

* The only name of a town which is masc., all others are neut.

MISCELLANEOUS PHRASES ON THE FOREGOING SECTIONS.

ive in town wohnen Sie in der Stadt

go into the country gehen Sie auf's Land

live always in the country leben Sie immer auf dem Lande

come here kommen Sie her

do not go there gehen Sie nicht hin

get into the carriage steigen[8] Sie in den Wagen

stand not so far off stehen Sie nicht so weit weg

stand[9] here under my umbrella stellen Sie sich hierher unter meinen Regenschirm

bring me a glass of water bringen Sie mir ein Glas[10] Wasser

fetch me a bottle of wine holen Sie mir eine Flasche Wein

take this plate away nehmen Sie diesen Teller weg

take this dish into the dining-room tragen (bringen[11]) Sie diese Schüssel in den Speisesaal

give him a cup of coffee geben Sie ihm eine Tasse Kaffee

drink a cup of tea trinken Sie eine Tasse Thee

eat a slice of bread and butter essen Sie eine Schnitte Butterbrod[12]

sleep half an hour schlafen Sie eine halbe Stunde (*lit.* a half hour)

do not sit on the grass sitzen Sie nicht auf dem Grase

---

[8] Steigen literally signifies to step or stride, and is therefore, according to the accompanying words, sometimes rendered by to ascend, sometimes by to descend.

[9] To stand is stehen, to cause, to stand to place or put stellen.

[10] *Of* between a substantive expressing measure, weight, or quantity, and another denoting a thing or things, without being followed by an article, pronoun or adjective, is not rendered.

[11] Bringen signifies both to bring and to take.

[12] Butterbrod means slices of bread with butter on them, but bread and butter, separately, is Brod und Butter.

MISCELLANEOUS PHRASES. 25

it down on this chair setzen Sie sich auf diesen Stuhl

do not lie on the table liegen Sie nicht auf dem Tisch

lie down on the sopha legen Sie sich auf das Sopha

do not make me laugh machen Sie mich nicht lachen

do not do that thun Sie das nicht

write a letter schreiben Sie einen Brief

sign my passport unterschreiben Sie meinen Paß

read this article lesen Sie diesen Artikel

sing this song singen Sie dieses Lied

look through this telescope sehen Sie durch dieses Fernrohr

hear her sing hören Sie sie singen

speak distinctly sprechen Sie deutlich

snuff the candle putzen Sie das Licht

let him clean your shoes lassen Sie ihn Ihre Schuhe putzen

do not make yourself too smart putzen [13] Sie sich nicht so sehr

go not yet to bed gehen Sie noch nicht zu Bette

do not get up yet stehen Sie noch nicht auf

wake me early wecken Sie mich früh

air my bed wärmen Sie mein Bett

air your room lassen Sie die Luft in Ihr Zimmer

leave the key in the lock lassen Sie den Schlüssel im Schlosse stecken

get the lock mended lassen [14] Sie das Schloß ausbessern

get my shirts washed lassen Sie meine Hemden waschen

have your handkerchiefs hemmed lassen Sie Ihre Schnupftücher säumen

---

[13] Putzen signifies the removal of any impurity; hence also, sich die Nase putzen to blow one's nose. It also signifies to make smart; hence, der Putz ornamental dress.

[14] All verbs expressing the causing of an action as in this and the four following phrases, are rendered by lassen (which here corresponds with the French *faire*) and is like that verb followed by an infin. active. *To send for* may also be expressed by holen lassen or kommen lassen.

make the boy go to school laſſen Sie den Knaben in die Schule gehen

send for a physician laſſen Sie einen Arzt rufen

I have a passport ich habe einen Paß

he has no pocket-book er hat keine Brieftaſche

we have our portmanteaus wir haben unſere Koffer

they have their travelling-bags ſie haben ihre Nachtſäcke

I go on board ich gehe an Bord

I land in the night ich lande in der Nacht

I get into the boat ich ſteige in das Boot

I send my luggage on shore ich ſchicke mein Gepäcke an's Land

I stay in the inn ich bleibe im Gaſthofe

I sleep on deck ich ſchlafe auf dem Verdecke

I am lying on my bed ich liege auf meinem Bette

I am just writing home ich ſchreibe eben nach Hauſe

he goes to town er geht in die Stadt

he lands before me er landet vor mir

she gets into a carriage ſie ſteigt in einen Wagen

he sends his letters to the post-office er ſchickt ſeine Briefe auf die Poſt

does she stay on board all night? bleibt ſie die ganze Nacht über an Bord?

does he not sleep in his cabin? ſchläft er nicht in ſeiner Kajüte?

she is lying on the sopha ſie liegt auf dem Sopha

he is just writing to England er ſchreibt eben nach England

we go on foot wir gehen zu Fuße

we are sitting at home wir ſitzen zu Hauſe

we travel by the diligence wir reiſen mit dem Eilwagen

we do not sleep in travelling wir ſchlafen nicht auf der Reiſe

you go to and fro Sie gehen auf und ab (hin und her)

you are sending too soon Sie schicken zu früh	he was in a hurry er war in Eile
you land on an island Sie landen auf einer Insel	she had no letters of introduction sie hatte keine Empfehlungsbriefe
do you not stay in the house? bleiben Sie nicht im Hause?	he travelled very fast er reisete sehr schnell
are you not writing home? schreiben Sie nicht nach Hause?	did he not send his luggage by the rail-road? schickte er nicht sein Gepäcke auf der Eisenbahn?
they are travelling by water sie reisen zu Wasser (zu Schiffe)	did she not land with her servants? landete sie nicht mit ihrer Dienerschaft?[16]
I was not quite satisfied ich war nicht ganz zufrieden	we were in no hurry wir waren in keiner Eile
I landed before all the rest ich landete vor allen übrigen	we had time enough wir hatten Zeit genug
I was (just) sending a messenger to you ich schickte Ihnen (eben)[15] einen Boten	the rain made us wet der Regen machte uns naß

the custom-house-officers searched our luggage die Zollbeamten durchsuchten unser Gepäcke	had you no contraband articles with you? hatten Sie nichts Verbotenes bei sich?
they were however very civil sie waren jedoch sehr höflich	did you travel merely for pleasure? reiseten Sie bloß zum Vergnügen?

---

[15] Eben is sometimes added to a sentence to express the identical moment, altho' *just* may not be contained in the equivalent English phrase.

[16] A collective singular, only used with reference to the house-hold of a person of station; otherwise we use Gesinde, also a coll. sing. A male servant (footman) is Bedienter; a maid-servant, Magd; a lady's maid, Kammerjungfer; a domestic servant, *generally*, der Dienstbote, plur. Dienstboten.

we have travelled merely for pleasure wir sind bloß zum Vergnügen gereiset

I have only travelled through France; but my cousin has travelled through all Europe ich bin bloß durch Frankreich gereiset; aber mein Vetter durch ganz Europa

we have sent them the maps wir haben ihnen die Landkarten geschickt

they have had a storm and have been in danger sie haben einen Sturm gehabt und sind in Gefahr gewesen

I had travelled in my own carriage ich war im eigenen Wagen gefahren

I had been greatly alarmed ich war sehr besorgt gewesen

had he not sent his brother the purse? hatte er nicht seinem Bruder die Börse geschickt?

she had long resided at the ambassador's sie hatte lange beim Gesandten gewohnt

we had been in the rain wir waren im Regen gewesen

we had had a stranger with us wir hatten einen Fremden bei uns gehabt

we had not been travelling fast enough wir waren nicht schnell genug gereiset

they had waked me before the time sie hatten mich vor der Zeit geweckt

had you not had a patron at court? hatten Sie nicht einen Beschützer am Hofe gehabt?

you had not ordered the post-horses Sie hatten die Postpferde nicht bestellt

I shall see his house and his garden ich werde sein Haus und seinen Garten sehen

I shall send you the goods from London to Munich ich werde Ihnen die Waaren von London nach München schicken

she will be astonished sie wird erstaunen

will the minister not sign my papers? wird der Minister nicht meine Papiere unterschreiben?

Yes, and you will find every thing in order to-morrow ja, und Sie werden morgen alles in Ordnung finden

the company will not separate yet die Gesellschaft wird noch nicht auseinander gehen

MISCELLANEOUS PHRASES.

we shall hear the young ladies sing, and see one play the harp wir werden die jungen Frauenzimmer singen hören und eine die Harfe spielen sehen

we shall stay a year on the continent wir werden ein Jahr auf dem Continente bleiben

we shall apprehend no danger wir werden keine Gefahr besorgen

you will then learn French and German and become very clever in these languages Sie werden alsdann Französisch und Deutsch lernen und in diesen Sprachen sehr geschickt werden

shall I not be ready? werde ich nicht fertig seyn?

he will have an answer er wird eine Antwort haben

she will take the news-papers into the study sie wird die Zeitungen in das Stubierzimmer (Cabinet) bringen

will he not be on Change? wird er nicht auf der Börse seyn?

we shall not remain alone in the counting-house wir werden nicht allein im Comptoir bleiben

we shall go together to the police-office wir werden zusammen auf's Polizeiamt gehen

we shall not be mis-informed there wir werden dort nicht falsch berichtet werden

you will *surely* not eat a pound of meat at once? sie werden doch nicht ein Pfund Fleisch auf einmal essen?

shall you take your chocolate without milk? werden Sie Ihre Chocolade ohne Milch trinken?

---

the lock of the portmanteau is broken das Schloß des Koffers (or am Koffer) ist zerbrochen

the leather of this travelling-bag is cracked das Leder dieses Reisesacks (or an diesem Reisesack) ist gesprungen

the size of that room does not suit me die Größe jenes Zimmers stehet mir nicht an

the colour of the chest was dark green die Farbe der Kiste (or an der Kiste) war dunkel-grün

the key of my desk was lost der Schlüssel meines Schreibpultes (or zu meinem Schreibpulte) war verloren

the quantity of his linen is prodigious die Menge seiner Wäsche (or Leinwand) ist ungeheuer the packing of your clothes gives you too much trouble das Einpacken Ihrer Kleider macht Ihnen zu viel Mühe

the name of this inn (hotel) was not known to me before der Name dieses Gasthofes war mir früher nicht bekannt

the bill of our host is tolerably reasonable die Rechnung unsers Wirthes ist ziemlich billig

the situation of yonder town is exceedingly picturesque die Lage jener Stadt dort ist höchst malerisch

it lies on the summit of a high and steep hill sie liegt auf dem Gipfel eines hohen und steilen Berges[17]

the affairs of the nation employ him constantly die Angelegenheiten der Nation beschäftigen ihn beständig

great courage deserves great praise großer Muth verdient großes Lob

good roads are agreeable for travelling gute Landstraßen sind angenehm zum Reisen

good coachmen are fond of strong horses gute Kutscher lieben starke Pferde

fine flowers do not always smell nice schöne Blumen riechen nicht immer gut

too bright light dazzles the eyes allzu helles Licht blendet die Augen

handsome people are not necessarily intelligent people schöne Menschen sind nicht nothwendig verständige Menschen

we have good new bread in the house wir haben gutes, frisches Brod im Hause

strong coffee and green tea are his favourite beverage starker Kaffee und grüner Thee sind seine Lieblingsgetränke

make some strong coffee and green tea machen Sie starken Kaffee und grünen Thee

I give the preference to roast meat above boiled ich gebe gebratenem Fleisch den Vorzug vor gekochtem

do you not give the preference to thick cream above common milk? geben Sie nicht dickem

---

[17] Hügel is used for a very small hill, or hillock.

Rahm den Vorzug vor gewöhn=
licher Milch?

ripe fruit is not unwholesome reifes
Obst ist nicht ungesund

we cannot preserve our health,
without pure air wir können
unsere Gesundheit nicht ohne reine
Luft erhalten

such wine gives one a head-ache
solcher Wein macht einem Kopf=
schmerzen

such beer is not drinkable solches
Bier ist nicht zu trinken

such milk easily turns sour solche
Milch wird leicht sauer

I hate such noise ich hasse sol=
chen Lärm

all noise annoys her aller Lärm ist
ihr zuwider

who can lift this stone? wer kann
diesen Stein heben?

none of us can do it keiner von
uns kann es thun

do you know any one of these
people? kennen Sie irgend einen[18]
von diesen Leuten?

I know not one of them ich kenne
nicht einen von ihnen

many a one has tried the experiment
mancher hat den Versuch gemacht

my new coachman is a foreigner
mein neuer Kutscher ist ein Aus=
länder

ADJECTIVES PRECEDED BY ARTICLES, ADJECTIVE PRONOUNS, OR OTHER ADJECTIVES.

the cold weather injures the young
crops die kalt=e Witterung schadet
der jung=en Saat

the new street is not far from the
old market die neu=e Straße ist
nicht weit von dem alt=en Markt

the British ambassador lives in
this long street der brittisch=e
Gesandte wohnt in dieser lang=en
Straße

he has a grown up son and a very
young daughter er hat einen
erwachsen=en Sohn und eine sehr
jung=e Tochter

I know the Austrian ambassador
very well ich kenne den öst(e)r=
reichisch=en Gesandt=en sehr gut

he is a very clever man er ist ein
sehr geschickt=er Mann

---

[18] *Any one*, *meaning of one kind or another* is rendered by irgend ein.

the new plan of that talented man has the approbation of all good people der neu=e Plan jenes talentvoll=en Mannes hat die Billigung aller gut=en Leute

you rate the importance of the new invention too highly Sie schlagen die Wichtigkeit der neu=en Erfindung zu hoch an.

you information is quite correct; but mine is not less so Ihre Nachricht ist ganz richtig; aber die meinig=e ist es nicht minder

I showed him my new apartments, and he showed me his ich zeigte ihm meine neu=en Zimmer, und er zeigte mir die sein=en

their new carriage was green, but ours was brown ihr neu=er Wagen war grün; aber der unsrig=e war braun

his whole fame arises from his singular connection with the prime minister sein ganz=er Ruhm entstehet aus seiner wunderlich=en Verbindung mit dem erst=en Minister

he ascribes it, however, to his own merit er schreibt ihn jedoch seinem eigen=en Verdienste zu

you have nothing left of your *nice cake*; will you have some of mine? Sie haben nichts von Ihrem schön=en Kuchen übrig; wollen Sie etwas von dem meinig=en haben?

the father was a good man der Vater war ein gut=er Mann

the mother was a good woman die Mutter war eine gut=e Frau

his brother was his best friend sein Bruder war sein best=er Freund

we were their best' friends wir waren ihre best=en Freunde

we presented the addresses to the young king and to the dowager queen wir überreichten die Addressen dem jung=en König und der verwittwet=en Königinn

he bought a very fine horse er kaufte ein sehr schön=es Pferd

strong beer does not agree with me stark=es Bier verträgt sich nicht mit mir

the taste of strong coffee and the smell of green tea are both disagreeable to her der Geschmack stark=en Kaffees und der Geruch grün=en Thees sind ihr beide zuwider

you do not doubt the wholesomeness of new milk and of new-laid eggs Sie bezweifeln nicht die Zuträglichkeit frisch-er Milch und frisch-er Eier

the frequent use of bad beer is hurtful der häufig-e Gebrauch schlecht-en Bieres (or von schlecht-em Biere) ist schädlich

the constant importation of salt butter makes the article cheap die beständig-e Einfuhr gesalzen-er Butter macht den Artikel wohlfeil

the many advantages of rich people are not to be denied die viel-en Vortheile reich-er Leute sind nicht zu läugnen

XXIV. Adjectives and adjective pronouns in the nom. sing. and in the acc. fem. and neut. preceded by the def. art. or by pronouns with the same ending as the def. art. add e.

In all other cases, when they follow an art. adj. pron. or adj., instead of repeating the terminations em, er or es, they take en.

XXV. When the subst. following a single adj. makes its gen. in s or es, the adj. in that case usually takes en, instead of es.

XXVI. As ein, kein etc., mentioned XI, c), and XII, b), p. 8 and 9, do not take er in the nom. masc. and es in the nom. and acc. neut.; the adjs. which follow them in those cases respectively take the er and es which they miss.

XXVII. Verbs compounded with a short prefix, such as be, emp, er, etc. or with any other particle not assuming the tonic accent, as well as those ending in iren or ieren do not take the prefix in the past participle.

XXVIII. Verbal prefixes having the tonic accent are, in the present, imperfect and imperative, removed to the end of the sentence, while the verb takes its usual position; but infinitives and participles are placed after them, the part. past taking ge, as usual.

Separable Compound Verbs.

open the window machen Sie das Fenster auf

shut the door machen Sie die Thüre zu

push the bolt schieben Sie den Riegel vor

unbolt the door riegeln Sie die Thüre auf.

have you opened the windows? haben Sie die Fenster aufgemacht?

have you not shut the doors haben Sie die Thüren nicht zugemacht

can you not unbolt the door können Sie nicht die Thür aufriegeln

bolt it now riegeln Sie sie jetzt zu

they get in at the window Sie steigen zum Fenster hinein

I come out of the door ich komme zur Thüre heraus

where will he come out? wo wird er heraus kommen?

where will she go in? wo wird sie hinein gehen?

we do not enter here into the church wir gehen nicht hier in die Kirche hinein

I go out ich gehe aus

he went out er ging aus

do not go out yet gehen Sie noch nicht aus

he will go out immediately er wird sogleich ausgehen

is she not gone out yet? ist sie noch nicht ausgegangen?

have you not to go out this morning? haben Sie diesen Morgen nicht auszugehen?

the bird flies away der Vogel fliegt weg

he has flown away er ist weggeflogen

he will never come back er wird niemals zurück kommen

do not let the children run out lassen Sie nicht die Kinder hinaus laufen

they will not run out of the house sie werden nicht zum Hause hinaus laufen

they have already run out sie sind schon hinaus gelaufen

do you see? they are just turning round, and will presently come in again sehen Sie? sie kehren so eben um, und werden gleich wieder herein kommen

the thieves entered by the window die Diebe stiegen zum Fenster hinein

we were in a carriage, and alighted before the door wir waren in einem Wagen und stiegen vor der Thüre aus he had been on horseback, but he had alighted before us er war zu Pferde gewesen, aber er war vor uns abgestiegen¹⁹

she went up stairs after me sie stieg nach mir die Treppe hinauf

they went down into the mine sie stiegen in das Bergwerk hinab

I have listened to her the whole evening ich habe ihr den ganzen Abend zugehört

you must attend Sie müssen aufmerken

I always attend ich merke immer auf

light my candle zünden Sie mein Licht an

do not snuff my light out putzen Sie mir nicht das Licht aus

has the servant lighted your fire? hat die Magd Ihr Feuer angezündet?

you must have a fire lighted in your bed-room Sie müssen ein Feuer in Ihrem Schlafzimmer anzünden lassen

who has put out my light? wer hat mein Licht ausgelöscht

I shall listen to the birds ich werde den Vögeln zuhören?

what are you copying? was schreiben Sie ab?

I am copying a poem ich schreibe ein Gedicht ab

PASSIVE VOICE.

what are they building? was bauet man?

they are building a church man bauet eine Kirche

the church is therefore building die Kirche wird also gebauet

the church is completed die Kirche ist vollendet

the church therefore is built die Kirche ist also gebauet

his tutor writes a book sein Hofmeister (Lehrer) schreibt ein Buch

a book is being written by his tutor ein Buch wird von seinem Lehrer geschrieben

---

* Aussteigen is an elliptical form for aus dem Wagen steigen, as einsteigen stands for in den Wagen steigen, aufsteigen for auf das Pferd steigen, and absteigen for von dem Pferde steigen.

the book is finished; it is written das Buch ist fertig; es ist geschrieben

the butcher killed an ox der Fleischer (Metzger) schlachtete einen Ochsen

the ox was slaughtered by the butcher der Ochse wurde von dem Fleischer geschlachtet

after he had been slaughtered by him, it was a slaughtered ox nachdem er von ihm geschlachtet worden war, war es ein geschlachteter Ochse

when I came, it was already slaughtered als ich kam, war er schon geschlachtet

is my fire lighted ist mein Feuer angezündet?

it has been lighted an hour ago by your servant es ist vor einer Stunde von Ihrem Bedienten angezündet worden

if it is not yet lighted, it shall be lighted presently wenn es noch nicht angezündet ist, so soll es sogleich angezündet werden

the general was taken prisoner after the battle der General wurde nach der Schlacht gefangen genommen

but he was soon again set at liberty aber er war bald wieder in Freiheit gesetzt

by whom was he liberated? von wem wurde er in Freiheit gesetzt?

he was liberated by a regiment of cavalry by means of a successful attack on the enemy's flank er wurde von einem Reiterregiment durch einen glücklichen Seitenangriff befreiet

was the dispatch not read, before you arrived? war die Depesche nicht gelesen, ehe Sie ankamen?

no; it was read in our presence nein, sie wurde in unserer Gegenwart gelesen

a tree is just being felled in my garden es wird so eben ein Baum in meinem Garten gefällt

the secret had not been betrayed by any one of the conspirators, but was discovered by a lost letter das Geheimniß war von keinem der Mitverschworenen verrathen worden, sondern[20] wurde durch einen verloren gegangenen Brief entdeckt

---

[20] *But* is commonly rendered by aber or allein; after a negation in opposition to that which is subsequently affirmed, by sondern; in the sense of *only*, through nur; *nothing but*, by nichts als.

XXIX. When the participle of a transitive verb joined to the auxiliary *to be* indicates *a state*, it is rendered by ſeÿn; but if it retains its original active sense, *to be* must be rendered by werden.

XXX. *By* relating to the person performing the action is translated by von; if to the *means* employed by a person, by durch.

XXXI. The usual place of the nom. in the indic. and subj. mood, if not interrogative, is at the beginning of a sentence and *immediately* before the verb. But in an interrogative sentence (unless the inter. pron. be itself the nom.), in the imperative, when *if* is understood, *and whenever the sentence commences with one word or more dependent on the verb*, the nom. is placed immediately *after* the verb.

XXXII. Sentences often begin with es merely with the object of drawing more attention to the verb (as *there* is frequently used in English), when the nom. is also placed after the verb.

XXXIII. The usual place of the verb (present or imperfect) is close to the nom.; but when a clause commences with a relative pron. or relative conjunction, the verb is moved to the end of the sentence.

XXXIV. When a clause commencing with wenn, da, als, and similar conjunctions, begins a period, the following clause usually commences with ſo.

Reflective Verbs.

how do you do? wie befinden Sie ſich?

I am very well ich befinde mich ſehr wohl

yesterday morning I was rather unwell geſtern Morgen befand ich mich etwas unwohl

how is Mr. N.— (your husband) wie befindet ſich Ihr Herr Gemahl

he is somewhat better than he has been for some weeks er befindet ſich etwas beſſer, als er ſich ſeit einigen Wochen befunden hat he will probably be better still to-morrow er wird sich wahrscheinlich Morgen noch besser befinden

there must be some of my things among your luggage es müssen sich einige von meinen Sachen unter Ihrem Gepäcke befinden

we found ourselves at once in a great crowd wir befanden uns auf einmal in einem großen Gedränge

I rejoice to see you ich freue mich (or es freuet mich) Sie zu sehen

he was rejoiced at your success er hat sich über Ihr Glück gefreuet

we shall rejoice to see him at our house after our return from the country wir werden uns (or es soll uns) freuen, ihn nach unserer Rückkehr (or Wiederkunft) vom Lande bei uns zu sehen

I am anxious to hear of them ich sehne mich, von ihnen zu hören

do not trouble yourself about me kümmern Sie sich nicht um mich

do not look round, till I call sehen Sie sich nicht um, bis ich rufe

I have looked for you every where ich habe mich überall nach Ihnen umgesehen

are you afraid to say it? fürchten Sie sich, es zu sagen?

try to recollect, whether you do not remember him besinnen Sie sich (doch), ob Sie sich seiner nicht erinnern

she grieved more for this good-for-nothing son than he deserved sie grämte sich mehr über diesen Taugenichts von einem Sohne, als er verdiente.

the matter must be decided very soon die Sache muß sich sehr bald entscheiden

I do not presume to decide thus upon the worth of a man ich maße mir nicht an auf diese Weise über den Werth oder Unwerth eines Menschen zu enscheiden

what do you imagine? was bilden Sie sich ein?

they imagined themselves to be people of importance sie bildeten sich ein wichtige Leute zu seyn

I am not conscious of being conceited by my advantages[21] ich bin mir nicht bewußt, mir etwas auf meine Vorzüge einzubilden

---

[21] *Advantage* in the sense of *gain* is der Vortheil, in that of *distinction*, der Vorzug.

REFLECTIVE VERBS.

thou didst not dare to approach the great man bu getrauteſt dir nicht, dich dem großen Manne zu nähern	he has resolved to request a favour er hat ſich vorgenommen, ſich eine Gunſt auszubitten
I dare every thing which is right in itself ich getraue mir alles, was an ſich ſelbſt recht iſt	the door seemed to close of its own accord die Thüre ſchien ſich von (ſich) ſelbſt zu ſchließen
what you have resolved upon cannot be done (is not feasible) was Sie ſich vorgenommen haben, läßt ſich nicht thun	the sky is getting over-cast with dark clouds der Himmel überzieht ſich mit trüben Wolken
nothing can be said against it es läßt ſich nichts dagegen ſagen	it is understood that you will not engage in the undertaking es verſtehet ſich, daß Sie ſich nicht in das Unternehmen einlaſſen
how was the business effected? wie machte ſich die Sache?	of course das verſteht ſich von ſelbſt
it was effected without trouble, as it were of its own accord ſie machte ſich ohne Mühe, wie von ſelbſt	such a business was not to be executed in a moment eine ſolche Angelegenheit ließ ſich nicht in einem Augenblick ausführen (or von der Hand ſchlagen)

XXXV. Many neuter verbs are in German conjugated with a reflective pronoun, showing that the action does not pass from the agent. Most of them require this pronoun in the acc., but some, in the dat.

XXXVI. Sometimes verbs are used reflectively instead of being joined to können to be able. Sometimes instead of the passive voice, in imitation of the French, where we must say *la porte se ferme*, instead of *fut fermée*, which would be the neuter form; while in German we may say, die Thüre ſchloß ſich instead of wurde geſchloſſen.

XXXVII. In speaking to persons of their relations, such as husband, wife, son, daughter etc., we do not, as in English, mention the person's name, as Mr. N., Mrs. N. Miss N, but Ihr Gatte or Gemahl,

Sohn, Oheim, Ihre Gattinn or Gemahlinn, Tochter, Tante, etc. To these, if we are not very intimate with the parties, we speak or write to, or they are our superiors, we prefix, to the male titles Herr, to those of married ladies Frau, to those of the unmarried, Fräulein. Thus Ihr Herr Vater, Ihre Frau Mutter, Ihr Fräulein Schwester.

XXXVIII. When the infinitive is not included in the same clause as the verb on which it depends, zu must be prefixed to it, which, in separable compound verbs, is placed after the compound particle.

XXXIX. Substantives of time or place, not preceded by prepositions, and answering to the question *when* or *where*, are put in the acc. case.

Impersonal or Uni-personal Verbs.

it thunders and lightens, it rains and snows, it hails and freezes all at the same time es donnert und blitzt, es regnet und schneiet, es hagelt und friert alles zu gleicher Zeit

it is frightful weather; I am cold all over es ist ein schreckliches Wetter; es friert mich am ganzen Leibe

yesterday it thawed, and I was quite hot gestern thauete es, und es war mir ganz heiß

now you are cold enough jetzt ist es Ihnen kalt genug

we were hungry and thirsty, but we were any thing but sleepy es hungerte und durstete uns; aber es schläferte uns keinesweges

they rejoiced to learn that he had succeeded in reaching the place of his destination so soon es freuete sie, daß es ihm gelungen war, seinen Bestimmungsort sobald zu erreichen

I have always repented having exerted myself so much[22] for him es hat mich immer gereuet, daß ich mich so sehr für ihn bemühet hatte

---

[22] *Much*, in relation to subst. is rendered by viel, but relating to verbs, by sehr.

IMPERSONAL OR UNI-PERSONAL VERBS. 41

I wonder that you repent of a good action es wundert mich, daß eine gute That Sie reuet

I am only vexed that I did it for so undeserving a person[23] es verdrießt mich nur, daß ich sie für einen so unwürdigen Menschen[24] ausübte

never repent of a good deed, done with a good intention Laſſen Sie ſich nie eine gute That, in guter Abſicht geübt, gereuen

what is your pleasure? was beliebt Ihnen?

I dreamt I was twenty pounds short of my money es träumte mir, mir fehlten Zwanzig Pfund von meinem Gelde

do not feel alarmed, your money is safe laſſen Sie es ſich nicht bange ſeyn, Ihr Geld iſt in Sicherheit

he wants courage, and he forbodes some great misfortune es gebricht ihm an Muth, und es ahnet ihm irgend ein großes Unglück

she is glad that your enterprize has not miscarried es iſt ihr lieb (or es freuete ſie), daß Ihr Unternehmen nicht mißlungen iſt

it is the same thing to them, whether he succeeds or fails es gilt Ihnen gleich, ob es ihm gelingt oder fehlſchlägt

I miss some of my papers es fehlen mir einige von meinen Papieren

when I looked down the precipice, I turned giddy, and I began to shudder als ich in den Abgrund hinunter blickte, ſchwindelte es mir (or ſchwindelte mir der Kopf), und es begann mir zu ſchaudern

I felt hot and cold by turns es wurde mir bald[25] heiß, bald kalt

if you are much concerned about the affair, I shall find it easy to gain information about it wenn Ihnen an der Sache viel liegt (or gelegen iſt), ſo wird (or ſoll) es mir leicht (or ein Leichtes) ſeyn, Belehrung (Auskunft) darüber zu erhalten

---

[23] Phrases like this must be translated with the art. before ſo or before the adj.; as, half the way der halbe Weg; so great an advance ein ſo großer Fortſchritt.

[24] Mensch means a human being, without regard to sex or age; Mann the male of the human race.

[25] Bald, soon, is used in this manner to express the English now, now this, now that, bald dieſes, bald jenes

I shall be pleased with all (that) you do alles, was Sie thun, wird (or soll) mir recht seyn

did you not find it difficult to get access to him? ist es Ihnen nicht schwer gefallen, Zutritt zu ihm zu erlangen?

I feel quite sultry in this room es ist mir ganz schwül in diesem Zimmer

If we do not open the windows, we shall all feel it sultry wenn wir nicht die Fenster aufmachen, wird es uns allen schwül werden

you are not faint, I hope es ist Ihnen hoffentlich nicht übel

O no, I am quite well o nein, mir ist ganz wohl

she seems poorly es scheint ihr nicht wohl zu seyn

I am quite well, as regards my health; but I feel ill at ease es ist mir ganz wohl, was meine Gesundheit betrifft; aber es ist mir schlimm zu Muthe

what are you alarmed at? vor was (or wovor) ist Ihnen bange?

I hear, my brother is very badly off ich höre, daß es meinem Bruder sehr schlecht geht

I am extremely sorry for it das thut mir äußerst leid

but I find it difficult to believe it aber es fällt mir schwer, es zu glauben

am I at liberty to go wherever I like? stehet es mir frei, zu gehen, wohin es mir beliebt?

yes, you are at liberty to do what you please ja, es stehet Ihnen frei, zu thun, was Ihnen beliebt

what are your feelings now? wie ist Ihnen jetzt zu Muthe?

I am in much better spirits now than I have been for some time es ist mir jetzt weit besser zu Muthe, als mir seit einiger Zeit gewesen ist

do you relish your meals? schmeckt Ihnen Ihr Essen?

I relish my dinner tolerably, but my breakfast I do not relish at all mein Mittagessen schmeckt mir ziemlich, aber mein Frühstück gar nicht

how do you relish (like) this wine? wie schmeckt Ihnen dieser Wein?

I do not taste it at all; I seem to have lost my power of tasting ich schmecke ihn gar nicht, mein Geschmackvermögen scheint mich verlassen zu haben

I formerly relished all equally ehemals schmeckte mir alles gleich gut	flowers were gathered, nosegays tied, songs were sung, every one was merry, and no one suspected any evil es wurden Blumen gebrochen, Sträuße gebunden, Lieder gesungen, alles war munter und guter Dinge, und niemandem ahnete (et) was Böses
I do not like to go to that house, there is nothing but eating and drinking going on there ich gehe nicht gern in jenes Haus, es wird dort nichts als gegessen und getrunken	
there was much laughing and joking, when I was there es wurde viel gelacht und gescherzt, als ich da war	I never dreamt that any thing would be said about it ich ließ es mir nie träumen, daß irgend etwas davon gesagt werden würde

XL. In the same manner as *it* is used in English, and *es* in German, to express an unknown or undefined agency for phenomena in external nature; *es* is also employed to express an undefined power, producing physical or moral changes within us, such as sleepiness, hunger, cold, heat, apprehension, astonishment, comfort, etc. The person acted on is then represented by the accusative or dative. The following require the accusative: —

dursten to be thirsty	schmerzen to grieve
sich freuen to rejoice	reuen to repent
frieren to be cold	wundern to wonder
hungern to be hungry	verdrießen to be vexed
schläfern to be sleepy	

The following require the dative: —

ahnen to forebode	fehlen, gebrechen, mangeln [26] to fail,
belieben to desire	to be in want

---

[26] These three verbs, when followed by *a n* signify not to be wanting, but *to miss*. Gebrechen is irregular, and conjugated like brechen; viz., es gebricht mir I want, es gebrach mir I wanted, es hat mir gebrochen I have wanted.

IMPERSONAL OR UNI-PERSONAL VERBS.

grauen to be horrified	wurmen to be annoyed
ankommen to come upon	gelingen to succeed
schaudern to shudder	mißlingen, fehlschlagen to fail
schwindeln to be giddy	schmecken to relish
träumen to dream	

Also the adjectives:—

angelegen concerned	recht right
bange alarmed	schlecht bad, ill
behaglich comfortable	schwer difficult
frei free	schlimm unwell
gut good	schwindlig giddy
heiß hot	übel ill, sick
kalt cold	warm warm
leicht easy	wohl well
leid sorry	unwohl unwell
lieb agreeable	

connected with the verbs seyn, werden, fallen, stehen, gehen, thun used with es; also wohl, schlimm, or nicht wohl zu Muthe, with seyn or werden.

XLI. There is also an impersonal possessive voice, which expresses actions performed by persons unknown or unstated, as shown in the last sentences just given.

XLII. Ich bin kalt, ich bin heiß means, I am of a cold or hot temperament; but es ist mir kalt or heiß I feel cold or hot.

XLIII. We may also say, ich bin hungrig, durstig, or schläfrig; or ich habe Hunger, Durst or Schlaf, for I am hungry, thirsty or sleepy.

XLIV. If the case governed by the impersonal verb is put before the verb, es is placed after the same, but more frequently omitted.

XLV. Lassen, as employed in several sentences in the foregoing *set of* phrases, has there its common signification of *to allow* or *permit.*

The Conditional.

I should relish every thing better, if I were well es würde mir alles besser schmecken, wenn ich gesund wäre

he would have succeeded much better, if he had gone to work more prudently es würde ihm viel besser geglückt (or gelungen) seyn, wenn er vorsichtiger zu Werke gegangen wäre.

I should gain my end for a certainty, if I followed your advice ich würde ganz sicherlich meinen Zweck erreichen, wenn ich Ihrem Rathe folgte

I should not have gained my end, even if I had followed your advice ich würde meinen Zweck nicht erreicht haben, selbst wenn ich Ihrem Rathe gefolgt hätte

should I have been expected, if I had not promised to come? würde ich erwartet worden seyn, wenn ich nicht versprochen hätte, zu kommen?

we should have determined to set off immediately, if we had had our pass-port wir würden uns entschlossen haben, sogleich abzureisen, wenn wir unsern Paß gehabt hätten

we should have set off before now, if the weather had not been so stormy wir würden schon vorlängst abgereist seyn, wenn das Wetter nicht so stürmisch gewesen wäre

if you had been determined to reach the continent so soon, you would not have minded the bad weather wenn Sie entschlossen gewesen wären, das Festland so bald zu erreichen, so würden Sie das schlechte Wetter nicht geachtet haben (or wären Sie entschlossen gewesen...., so hätten Sie das schlechte Wetter nicht geachtet)

they would not travel by the railway, if speed were not an object with them sie würden nicht auf der Eisenbahn reisen, wenn Schnelligkeit nicht ein wichtiger Punkt bei ihnen wäre

XLVI. The conditional is formed by means of the imperf. subj. of werden; viz., ich or er würde, du würdest, wir or sie würden, ihr würdet, with the infinitive, present or past, in the same manner as the future. Sometimes the imperfect subj. of the verb to be conjugated is used instead, as, ich wäre or ich hätte for ich würde seyn or ich würde haben.

XLVII. The only difference between the subj. and indicative is, that in the present tense the former always makes the third person singular in e, while the latter has t or et, and the imperfect subj. in *irregular* verbs changes the vowels a, o, or u of the imperfect indicative into ä, ö, or ü, and adds the e to the first and third person sing. wanting in the latter.

XLVIII. The subjunctive is chiefly employed to express suppositions and contingencies; but also to quote things stated by ourselves or by others indirectly, without our using the exact words employed. Thus, a person told you, I am glad to see you; if you mention this, you may either say: He told me, I am glad to see you —or: He was glad to see me; and this must be rendered by the subjunctive er freue, or er freuete sich. The present may be used, if the words alluded to were used in that tense; but the imperfect is often employed even then, especially if it expresses the mood more clearly than the present.

PREPOSITIONS

Of Locality, without Motion.

a) *Governing the Genitive.*

outside außerhalb*	on this side dießseit
inside innerhalb	on that side jenseit
above oberhalb	not far from unweit
below unterhalb	

---

* From halb in its ancient signification of *side.*

PREPOSITIONS OF LOCALITY. 47

    b) *Governing the Dative.*

out of außer   at in, zu
near, close to bei, zunächst   opposite gegenüber
above ob (for oberhalb)

    c) *Governing the Accusative.*
     round um

  OF LOCALITY, WITH MOTION.

    a) *Governing the Dative.*

to (a person or thing) zu, (a place)   towards or in opposition entgegen
nach   contrary, against zuwider

    b) *Governing the Accusative.*

  towards, against gegen (gen), wider

OF LOCALITY, EXPRESSIVE BOTH OF REST AND OF MOTION;
GOVERNING IN THE FORMER THE DATIVE, AND IN THE LATTER
THE ACCUSATIVE.

on, at, near to an   behind hinter
on (upon) auf   by the side of neben
above über   in ⎫
below unter   into ⎬ in
before vor   ⎭
            between zwischen

---

the best hotel of this town lies outside the town, on the other side of the river der beste Gasthof dieser Stadt liegt außerhalb der Stadt, jenseit des Flusses

I would rather sleep inside the town, and this side the bridge ich wollte (or möchte) lieber innerhalb der Stadt und diesseit der Brücke schlafen

the consul lives within a park above the town-house, not far from the police-office der Consul wohnt innerhalb eines Parkes, oberhalb des Stadthauses, unweit des Polizeiamtes (or nicht weit von dem Polizeiamte)

the steam-boat always lands below the custom-house das Dampfboot legt immer unterhalb des Zollhauses an

---

out of society such things may be tolerated außer der Gesellschaft lassen sich solche Dinge dulden

out of the house you may make as much noise as you like außer dem Hause mögen Sie so viel Lärm machen, als Sie wollen

you sit near my oldest friend Sie sitzen bei meinem ältesten Freunde

the farm-house lies close by the road-side der Pachthof liegt dicht bei der Landstraße

he was killed in the battle of Jena er wurde in der Schlacht bei Jena getödtet (or er kam in der Schlacht bei Jena um [27])

who sat next to you? wer saß Ihnen zunächst?

the village lay above the forest das Dorf lag ob dem Walde

Napoleon was at that time still at Moscow Napoleon war zu jener Zeit (or um jene Zeit, or damals) noch (immer [28]) in Moskau

at Milan things go on differently zu Mailand geht es anders her

they are hardly ever at home sie sind fast nie zu Hause

at my feet lay a broken watch zu meinen Füßen lag eine zerbrochene (Taschen)uhr

---

[27] Um etwas kommen to lose (be deprived of something); einen um etwas bringen to take something from a person. Um das Leben kommen to lose life, to perish; um das Leben bringen to deprive of life, to kill, are both frequently used in the same sense, without das Leben, in the form of umkommen, umbringen.

[28] Immer after noch expresses continuity, *he continued to stay.*

the young lady wore a wreath of white roses round her head die junge Dame (or das junge Frauenzimmer) trug einen Kranz von weißen Rosen um den Kopf

the military drew a *cordon* round the infected district die Truppen zogen ein Cordon (einen Kreis) um die an der Ansteckung leidende (or inficirte) Gegend

---

to whom are you going? zu wem gehen Sie?

the children ran to their uncle die Kinder liefen zu ihrem Oheim (or Onkel)

will you come this evening to our house (to our party)? wollen Sie heute Abend zu uns (zu unserer Gesellschaft) kommen?

to whom (to whose house) are you invited? zu wem sind Sie eingeladen?

to what were they invited? zu was waren sie eingeladen?

we invited them to dinner wir luden sie zum (Mittag)essen ein

we shall go to the next representation of the "Huguenots" wir werden zur nächsten Vorstellung der Hugenotten gehen

send the whole to my hotel (house, lodging) schicken Sie alles zusammen nach meinem Gasthofe (Hause, Logis, Quartier; nach meiner Wohnung)

Put this coat with (to) the rest of my clothes legen Sie diesen Rock zu meinen übrigen Sachen

when shall you set off for (to) Leghorn? wann werden Sie nach Livorno abreisen?

he went with the first train to Liege er ging mit dem ersten (Wagen)zuge nach Lüttich

I will take both the maps and charts home with me ich werde sowohl die Land- als die Seekarten mit nach Hause nehmen

every thing is against me alles ist mir entgegen

the senate solemnly met the triumpher der Senat zog dem Triumphator feierlich entgegen

as often as I return home, my dog always runs to meet me so oft ich nach Hause zurückkomme, läuft mir mein Hund immer entgegen

all (that) I eat disgusts me alles, was ich esse, ist mir zuwider

E

when I entered the room, several couples met me dancing als ich in den Saal[29] trat, tanzten mir mehrere Paare entgegen[30] (or kamen mir mehrere Paare entgegengetanzt)

even his own brothers acted against and opposed him selbst seine leiblichen Brüder handelten ihm zuwider und arbeiteten ihm entgegen

it was so dark that I ran against a post es war so dunkel, daß ich gegen einen Pfosten rannte

---

the table stands by (against) the wall, and several of them sit at it der Tisch steh(e)t an der Wand, und mehrere von ihnen sitzen daran (or an demselben)

how many pictures were there hanging against the walls? wie viele Gemälde hingen an den Wänden?

they hung the pictures against the wall sie hingen die Gemälde an die Wand

I hope the wind will not be against them ich hoffe, der Wind werde (or wird) ihnen nicht zuwider seyn

if you want to see the sun rise, you must turn towards the east wenn Sie die Sonne wollen aufgehen sehen, so müssen Sie sich gen Osten wenden

can you swim against the stream? können Sie wider den Strom schwimmen?

the whole world is against me die ganze Welt ist wider mich

place the table against the wall, and sit down at it stellen Sie den Tisch an die Wand und setzen Sie sich an denselben (daran)

what lies on the chair? was liegt auf dem Stuhle?

what have you laid on the sofa? was haben Sie auf das Sopha gelegt?

who has sat on the sofa? wer hat auf dem Sopha gesessen?

---

[29] Saal means a large room; Zimmer a common-sized room, as is usually had for a sitting or a bed room. In some parts of Germany Stube is preferred to Zimmer.

[30] Entgegen may be joined to almost every verb of action with which an *individual* may be met, and is always treated like a separable particle.

be so good (as) to sit down on the sofa seyn Sie so gütig sich auf das Sopha zu setzen (or niederzulassen)

over the looking-glass hung a green silk curtain über dem Spiegel hing ein grün-seidener Vorhang

you must hang another curtain over the looking-glass Sie müssen einen andern Vorhang über den Spiegel hängen

did the dog not lie under the staircase? lag der Hund nicht unter der Treppe?

the footman put the letter under the hall-door der Bediente steckte den Brief unter die Hausthüre

the farmer's son has served among the French troops in Algiers des Pächters Sohn hat unter den französischen Truppen in Algier gedient

do you know how he got among them? wissen Sie, wie er unter sie gerieth?

before the church stands a beautiful lime-tree vor der Kirche stehet ein schöner Lindenbaum

who has put this flower-pot before the window? wer hat diesen Blumentopf vor das Fenster gestellt?

I found it too hot in my study, and went outside the door ich fand es in meinem Studierzimmer zu heiß und ging vor die Thüre

I walked up and down before the door ich spazierte vor der Thüre auf und ab

what tribe lives behind the mountain? welcher Volksstamm wohnt hinter dem Berge?

as the pasture in the valley on this side was insufficient for their flocks, they moved behind the range da die Weide in dem Thale auf dieser Seite nicht für ihre Heerden hinreichte, so zogen sie hinter das Gebirge

nor have they ever returned into the valley auch sind sie niemals wieder in das Thal zurückgekehrt

between the one and the other I was ill advised zwischen dem einen und dem andern ward ich schlecht berathen

he settled between two rivers er ließ sich zwischen zweien Flüssen nieder

stand between those two shrubs stellen Sie sich zwischen jene zwei Stauden

XLIX. Es is often used for *somebody* or *something*, as Schiller says in the Taucher: es wallet, und siedet, und brauset und zischt it (something in the water) boils, and seethes, and roars, and hisses.

L. Zu expresses *at* a place, in, *in* a country.

LI. If several compound words come in succession, the last member of which is common to all, it is usually given but once; thus for Landkarten maps, and Seekarten charts, Land= und Seekarten.

LII. In compound substantives the first word expresses the quality, use, time, manner of the last. If, therefore, the former is otherwise known, it is often omitted. Thus Uhr means an instrument for determining the hours; therefore we say for watch Taschenuhr (pocket-time-piece), for clock Schlaguhr (striking time-piece), for repeater Repetieruhr, for church-clock Kirchenuhr, for table-clock Standuhr, for sun-dial Sonnenuhr, for hour-glass Sanduhr. But we say generally, wie viel Uhr ist es? what o'clock is it? or, if it is understood of what time-piece we are speaking, geht Ihre Uhr gut? wie viel ist es auf Ihrer Uhr? does your watch (or clock) go well? how much is it by your watch (or clock)? Or, das Mittagsessen the dinner, das Abendessen the supper, zu Mittag essen to dine, zu Abend essen to sup. But if we say: essen Sie bei uns, without mentioning a time, it would be understood to mean, Take your principal meal, or dine, with us. Die Landreise journey, die Seereise voyage; Land= und Seereisen travels and voyages; er ist auf Reisen he is on his travels; er hat eine Reise nach Amerika gemacht he has made a *voyage* to America.

LIII. *Which* in the accusative, often omitted in English, must always be expressed in German.

LIV. *Of* after pronouns and the superlative of adjectives is usually rendered by von (followed by the dative.)

PREPOSITIONS OF TIME.

Governing the Genitive.

während whilst, while

PREPOSITIONS OF ORIGIN, CAUSE, AND CONSEQUENCE.

while we are speaking, the time passes während wir sprechen, vergeht die Zeit.

Governing the Dative.

binnen within

seit[31] since

within a week, all was settled binnen acht Tagen war alles abgemacht

since when have you been here? seit wann sind Sie schon hier?

I have been in town since the beginning of last[32] month ich bin schon seit dem Anfange des vorigen Monats in der Stadt

LV. When speaking of a time *still continuing*, we use in German the present, instead of the perfect, adding the adverb schon, already. The perfect expresses a time indefinitely, or lately past.

PREPOSITIONS OF ORIGIN, CAUSE, AND CONSEQUENCE.

Governing the Genitive.

halben or halber on account
kraft by virtue
laut according

um ..... willen for the sake
vermöge by dint
wegen concerning, on account

on whose account (or on what account) do you propose to undertake this long journey? weff(ent)halben beabsichtigen Sie diese lange Reise vorzunehmen?

on account of the business which, by virtue of my office, I have to investigate wegen des Geschäftes, welches ich, kraft meines Amtes, zu untersuchen habe

---

[31] The adverb *since* is seitdem; as, since you have been in town seitdem Sie in der Stadt gewesen sind.

[32] *Last* is rendered by letzt, when it means the end of a series; but by vorig, when it means a period past before the present one in question.

on account of acquaintanceship alone I would not have undertaken it Bekanntschaft halber[33] allein würde ich sie nicht unternommen haben

according to the tenour of our orders[34] we must press for the payment of the bill[35] laut des Inhalts unserer Aufträge müssen wir auf die Zahlung des Wechsels bringen

for whose sake have they interfered in the matter? um wessentwillen haben sie sich in die Sache gemischt?

they have certainly not done it for my sake sie haben es gewiß(lich) nicht um meinetwillen gethan

you do these things for the sake of appearance Sie thun diese Dinge um des Scheines willen

I wish to call on him entirely for your sake ich wünsche ihn gänzlich um Ihretwillen zu besuchen

as far as I am concerned, you may do it, or let it alone meinethalben mögen Sie es thun, oder es bleiben lassen

for heaven's sake, make yourself not ridiculous! um's Himmels willen, machen Sie sich nicht lächerlich!

he ruled the nation by dint of his strength of will er beherrschte die Nation vermöge seiner Willenskraft

on what account was he banished the country? weßwegen wurde er des Landes verwiesen?

was it on our account? war (or geschah) es unseretwegen?

he was banished solely on account of his connection with the late conspiracy er wurde einzig wegen seiner Verwickelung in die neuliche Verschwörung verwiesen

---

[33] Without an article before the substantive we say halber instead of halben.

[34] *Order* (arrangement) die Ordnung, (command) der Befehl, (direction) der Auftrag, (of knighthood or monkery) der Orden, (in a bill of exchange) die Ordre.

[35] *Bill* (of exchange) der Wechsel, (reckoning) die Rechnung, (of parliament) der Gesetzvorschlag, die Bill, (beak) der Schnabel.

Governing the Dative.

aus out of, from
von of, from

gemäß according

---

the whole mistake arose from a fancy of our late minister [36] der ganze Irrthum entſtand aus einem Wahn unſeres verſtorbenen Pfarrers

I know from experience that it will be too late to apply ich weiß aus Erfahrung, daß es zu ſpät ſeyn wird, anzufragen

the landlord turned the troublesome guests out of the house der Wirth warf die unruhigen Gäſte zum Hauſe hinaus

it is now a long time, since I lost sight of your old acquaintance es iſt nun ſchon lange her, ſeitdem ich Ihren alten Bekannten aus den Augen verloren habe

out of sight, out of mind, is a common proverb and a common truth aus den Augen, aus dem Sinn, iſt ein gemeines Sprüchwort und eine allgemeine Wahrheit

you will have perceived from my last communication, that I was then at Naples Sie werden aus meiner letzten Mittheilung erſehen haben, daß ich mich damals (or zur Zeit) zu Neapel befand

I can prove it from holy writ ich kann es aus der heiligen Schrift beweiſen

I should know him again out of a thousand ich würde ihn aus tauſend Menſchen wieder erkennen

translate this essay from English into German, without a dictionary überſetzen Sie dieſen Aufſatz aus dem Engliſchen in's Deutſche ohne Wörterbuch

do you come straight from home? kommen Sie geraden Weges von Hauſe?

at what o'clock did the stranger go from you? um wie viel Uhr ging der Fremde von Ihnen (weg)?

---

[36] *Minister* in its primitive sense is Diener; in the church, Pfarrer, Prediger, Geiſtlicher; in the state, Miniſter, Staatsminiſter.

they were armed from head to foot sie waren vom Kopf bis auf die Füße bewaffnet

for a long time after, I felt from time to time a throbbing in my left thumb noch lange nachher fühlte (or empfand) ich von Zeit zu Zeit ein Schlagen in dem linken Daumen

I received these prints[37] direct from Venice ich empfing diese Kupferstiche unmittelbar von Venedig

from him and his skill I expect every thing von ihm und von seiner Geschicklichkeit erwarte ich Alles

from whom have you learnt Italian? von wem haben Sie Italienisch (or das Italienische) gelernt?

the slater fell from the roof der Schieferdecker fiel vom Dache

he was possessed of a notion that he would be devoured by wild beasts er war von einem Gedanken besessen, daß er würde von wilden Thieren gefressen werden

you will have to suffer much from the heat Sie werden viel von der Hitze zu leiden haben

deduct five from seven ziehen Sie fünf von sieben ab

from that period she withdrew her hand from her niece von jener Zeit an zog sie ihre Hand von ihrer Nichte ab

the smoke seems to come from up stairs der Rauch scheint von oben herunter (or herab) zu kommen

from what language do you derive this word? von welcher Sprache leiten Sie dieses Wort ab (or her)?

from that time forward he was an altered man von da an war er ein andrer Mensch

henceforward you may receive any present from him (which) he may choose to offer (to) you von nun an mögen Sie jedes Geschenk von ihm annehmen, das er Ihnen anbieten mag (or dürfte)

---

[37] *Print* (copy of an engraving) der Kupferstich, (in relation to the appearance of the print as to the striking off) der Abdruck, (the style in which a book is *printed*) der Druck, (calico) der Kattun; printed gedruckt; printed silk gedruckte Seide.

PREPOSITIONS OF ORIGIN, CAUSE, AND CONSEQUENCE.

he promised us to write to us from Vienna, but he only wrote from Buda er verſprach uns, uns von Wien aus zu ſchreiben, aber er ſchrieb erſt von Ofen aus

she has had this habit of blushing from childhood ſie hat dieſe Gewohnheit zu erröthen ſchon von Kindheit auf

this custom has reached us from ancient times dieſer Gebrauch iſt von Alters her auf uns (herab)gekommen

my patron is of an ancient family mein Gönner ſtammt von einer alten Familie ab

will you have it of gold or silver? wollen Sie es von Gold oder Silber haben?

all your coats are made of the finest cloth alle Ihre Röcke ſind von dem feinſten Tuche gemacht

he acted quite in conformity with his known character er handelte (or verfuhr) gänzlich ſeinem bekannten Character gemäß

LVI. Adjectives, declined in the neuter gender, are often used as abstract substantives. Of this nature are words like das Italieniſche, das Engliſche, das Deutſche, etc., which are employed instead of die italieniſche, engliſche, deutſche Sprache the Italian, English, German language.

LVII. An, auf, or her are placed after substantives and closely joined to them in pronunciation, as a complement to von, when it means from (a place or time); which otherwise might be supposed to mean *about* or *concerning*. Thus, er ſchrieb von Wien, he wrote concerning Vienna.

Governing the Genitive, if preceding, and the Dative, if following the Noun.

in obedience, according zufolge

according to the report current to-day on change, war has been declared between Russia and the Porte zufolge des Gerüchtes, welches heute auf der Börſe im Umlaufe war, iſt zwiſchen Rußland und der Pforte Krieg erklärt worden

in obedience to your orders conveyed in your favour of the 18th inst., I have shipped to your account 800 quarters of wheat Ihrem Auftrage zufolge, welcher mir in Ihrem Geehrten (Schreiben) vom 18ten dieses (Monats) zugekommen ist, habe ich acht hundert Quarter Weizen für Ihre Rechnung verschifft (or verladen)

Governing the Accusative.
for (for the sake of) um

he sued for this young lady's hand er warb (or bewarb sich) um die Hand dieses Fräuleins

do not trouble yourself for (about) me bekümmern Sie sich nicht um mich

I beg for your friendship, not for your interest at court ich bitte um Ihre Freundschaft, nicht um Ihren Einfluß bei Hofe

they play for money sie spielen um Geld

LVIII. The following prepositions may be placed indifferently before or after the substantive without altering their government: halben or halber, ungeachtet, wegen, gegenüber (or gegen before, and über after it, like um .... willen).

LIX. The following are always placed after the substantives: entgegen, gemäß, entlang, zunächst, zuwider; also nach when it signifies *along* or *according*, and durch when it means *during*.

Prepositions of Connection.
(All governing the Dative.)

besides außer, nächst, nebst
by, near, with bei

with mit
together with mit

besides (after) him I know no one whom I esteem more nächst ihm kenne ich niemanden, den *ich mehr schätze*

besides me no one knew the officer außer mir kannte niemand den Offizier besides the governor of the Bank of England there were the chairmen of all the English and Scotch railway-companies nebſt dem Gouverneur (or Director) der Bank von England waren alle die Präſidenten (or Vorſteher) aller engliſchen und ſchottiſchen Eiſenbahnen da

who was that who sat next to you? wer war es, der bei Ihnen ſaß?

you have a beautiful oak standing close by your gate Sie haben eine herrliche Eiche dicht bei Ihrem Thore ſtehen

have you any change about you? haben Sie (kein) klein Geld bei ſich?

I have nothing but gold about me ich habe nichts als Goldſtücke bei mir

under these circumstances, nothing was left to me but to submit bei (also unter) dieſen Umſtänden blieb mir nichts übrig, als mich zu unterwerfen

can you hear with this noise? können Sie bei dieſem Lärm hören?

In a thunder storm it is dangerous to stand under a tree bei einem Gewitter iſt es gefährlich unter einem Baume zu ſtehen

with such a storm it would be madness to go to sea bei einem ſolchen Sturme wäre es Tollheit (or Raſerei), auf's Meer zu gehen

with us this coin is not current bei uns gilt dieſe Münze nicht

with me your excuses will not take bei mir ſchlagen Ihre Entſchuldigungen (or Ausreden) nicht an

dine with me at Verey's ſpeiſen Sie mit mir bei Verey

I came to an understanding with my cousin that we should together with our aunt go to Bennet's concert ich kam mit meiner Couſine[38] überein, daß wir nebſt unſrer Tante nach Bennet's Concert gehen ſollten

LX. *Any* in interrogations is often omitted, frequently also rendered by kein no.

LXI. Klein Geld (undeclined) means change, kleines Geld small money.

---

[38] Couſine or Baſe, a female cousin; Vetter, male cousin.

Governing the Genitive. —Instead ſtatt, anſtatt
——————— *Accusative.*—For für

will you go there instead of them? wollen Sie ſtatt (anſtatt) ihrer (or an ihrer Statt) hingehen?	for whom do you interest yourself most? für wen intereſſiren Sie ſich am meiſten?
Instead of the husband, the wife came ſtatt des Gatten (or Mannes) kam die Gattinn (or Frau)	do for others what you wish that others should do for you thun Sie für andere, was Sie wünſchen, das andere für Sie thun ſollten
do not be afraid for me für mich ſorgen Sie nicht	

PREPOSITIONS OF INSTRUMENTALITY.

Governing the Genitive. —By means mittels, mittelſt, vermittelſt
——————— *Accusative.*—Through durch

I shall inform you in the right time by means of a special messenger ich werde Sie zur rechten Zeit mittels eines eigenen Boten (or Couriers) in Kenntniß ſetzen	the theft was discovered through a mere accident der Diebſtahl wurde durch einen bloßen Zufall entdeckt
the thieves opened the iron safe by means of a crow-bar die Diebe erbrachen die eiſerne Kiſte mittelſt eines Brecheiſens	fortunes are more frequently made through small economies than through large gains Leute werden öfter durch kleine Erſparniſſe als durch große Gewinſte reich

PREPOSITIONS OF RESTRICTION.

Governing the Genitive. —Notwithstanding ungeachtet
——————— *Dative.* —Except nächſt; in spite trotz
——————— *Accusative.*—Without ohne, ſonder (rather obsolete)

notwithstanding all your efforts, you will not make this foolish youth either wiser or better ungeachtet aller Ihrer Bemühungen werden Sie diesen thörichten Jüngling (or jungen Menschen) weder weiser noch besser machen

in spite of you, he will remain what he is trotz Ihnen wird er bleiben, was er ist

I shall be sorry, if it shall prove so, since, besides me, he has no relation, and stands without one friend in the world es soll mir leid thun, wenn es sich so erweiset; da er nächst mir keinen Verwandten hat und ohne einen einzigen Freund in der Welt bastehet

LXII. The Present is sometimes used for the Future, if the time is in close proximity.

LXIII. Ein is often followed by einzig, the two together signifying *one*, while ein alone, also means *a*.

LXIV. Kraft is literally *power*.
Laut comes from lauten *to sound*.
Mittels, etc., from die Mitte *middle*, das Mittel *the means*; hence vermitteln to mediate, to bring about.
Um...willen *for the will*.
Ungeachtet, from achten to esteem, to mind—*unmindful*.
Vermöge from vermögen *to be able*.
Während, part. pres. of währen *to continue, endure*.
Wegen is connected with Weg *way—through the way*.
Gegenüber *over against*.
Gemäß from messen *to measure*.
Sammt, from an old verb, the root of sammeln *to collect*.
Trotz from trotzen *to defy*.
Zufolge from folgen *to follow*.
Sonder from sondern *to separate*.

"Of" rendered by Prepositions.

the kings of England of the house of Brunswick have often made some of their British subjects knights of the Guelphic order die Könige von England aus dem Hause Braunschweig haben oft einige von ihren brittischen Unterthanen zu Rittern des Guelphen (or Welfen)=Ordens gemacht

the emperor of Austria is at the same time king of Hungary and Lombardy, duke of Tyrol and count of Habsburg der Kaiser von Oest(er)reich ist zu gleicher Zeit König von Ungarn und der Lombardei, Herzog von Tyrol und Graf von Habsburg

the climate of Italy is various das Klima von Italien ist mannigfaltig

the extent of ancient Rome is not easily determined die Größe (or Ausdehnung) des alten Rom ist nicht leicht zu bestimmen

after many difficulties and dangers the frigate safely made the port of Alexandria nach manchen Schwierigkeiten und Gefahren lief die Fregatte glücklich in den Hafen von Alexandrien ein

the commander of an army of 100,000 men requires more caution and circumspection than the captain of a company der Befehlshaber eines Heeres von hundert tausend Mann bedarf mehr Vor= und Umsicht als der Hauptmann einer Compagnie

various people have various kinds of antipathies verschiedene Leute haben verschiedene Arten von Widerwillen

some cannot bear the sight of a toad, others the taste of apples, others the smell of roses, some again the touch of velvet einige können den Anblick einer Kröte nicht ertragen, andere den Geschmack von Aepfeln, andere den Geruch von Rosen, einige wieder die Berührung von Sammt

steeples of 300 feet high are not very uncommon; as little as ships of 3,000 tons Kirch(en)thürme von dreihundert Fuß Höhe sind nicht sehr selten (or nichts sehr seltenes); eben so wenig als Schiffe von drei tausend Tonnen

you may see by this cross of diamonds which he wears on his breast that he is a man of rank Sie können (es) an dem Kreuze von Diamanten, das er auf der Brust trägt, sehen, daß er ein Mann von Stande ist

a man of such high merit may fairly claim the hand of a lady of good family ein Mann von solch hohem Verdienste darf billig auf die Hand eines Frauenzimmers (or einer Dame) von guter Familie Anspruch machen

I have lately lost a beautiful horse of 14 hands high and of only four years ich habe neulich ein herrliches Pferd von vierzehn Faust Höhe und von nur vier Jahren verloren

she has married a youth of 20 years of age sie hat einen Jüngling von zwanzig Jahren (or einen zwanzigjährigen Jüngling) geheirathet

the neighbourhood of Liége is hilly die Gegend um Lüttich (her) (or die Umgegend von Lüttich) ist bergig

the love of life is implanted in man die Liebe zum Leben ist dem Menschen eingepflanzt

children ought to be trained to a habit of obedience and self-government Kinder sollten zur Gewöhnung zum Gehorsam und zur Selbstbeherrschung angeleitet werden

is it not strange that the desire of accumulating should be more peculiar to old age than to youth? ist es nicht sonderbar, daß die Lust anzuhäufen mehr dem Alter als der Jugend eigen seyn sollte?

nothing but the fear of offending restrained me nichts als die Furcht zu beleidigen hielt mich zurück

every thing depends on the mode of doing it alles hängt von der Art es zu thun (or wie man es thut) ab

the prospect of gaining wealth and fame drove him into this ruinous war die Aussicht Reichthum und Ruhm zu erwerben, trieb (or stürzte) ihn in diesen verderblichen Krieg

the hope of immortality has always been an incentive to great deeds die Hoffnung auf Unsterblichkeit ist zu allen Zeiten ein Antrieb zu großen Thaten gewesen the mere enjoyment of existence is a high degree of happiness die bloße Luft am Daseyn ist ein hoher Grad von Glück (or Seligkeit)

the praise-worthy wish of pleasing should never degenerate into coquetry der lobenswerthe Wunsch zu gefallen sollte nie in die Sucht zu gefallen (or Gefallsucht) ausarten

love of men is called in English after the Greek, philanthropy, and in German by a compound word Liebe zu den Menschen wird im Englischen, nach dem Griechischen, Philanthropie, und im Deutschen mit einem zusammengesetzten Worte (Menschenliebe) genannt

the fear of God is called — die Furcht vor Gott nennt man Gottesfurcht

the fear of death — die Furcht vor dem Tode, Todesfurcht

the fear of water, hydrophobia die Scheu vor dem Wasser, Wasserscheu

the rage of (for) gambling — die Sucht zu spielen, die Spielsucht

the want of money — der Mangel an Geld, der Geldmangel

the want of water — der Mangel an Wasser, der Wassermangel

the fear of ghosts — die Furcht vor Gespenstern, die Gespensterfurcht

the hatred of (towards) men — der Haß gegen die Menschen, der Menschenhaß

the danger of (through) fire — die Gefahr durch das Feuer, die Feuersgefahr

the distress of (by) water (inundation), or of (by) hunger — die Noth durch das Wasser oder den Hunger, die Wassersnoth, die Hungersnoth

the thirst of gold — der Durst nach Gold, der Goldburst

you find esteem of virtue even among the vicious man findet Achtung vor der Tugend selbst unter den Lasterhaften

my neighbour's dread of mad dogs makes him tremble at every dog (which) he meets meines Nachbars Angst vor tollen Hunden läßt ihn vor jedem Hunde zittern, dem er begegnet

derision of a fallen enemy betrays a vulgar mind Spott über einen gefallenen Feind verräth eine gemeine Gesinnung

in our mad pursuit of pleasure we forget but too often all thought of danger in unferm tollen Streben nach Vergnügen vergessen wir nur zu oft jeden Gedanken an Gefahr

his disgust of every useful occupation necessarily ruined him fein Ekel vor jedweder nützlichen Beschäftigung richtete ihn nothwendiger Weise zu Grunde

LXV. Von is often used as a substitute for the genitive, when the word is not preceded by an article, adjective, or pronoun, in which the case could be marked; especially before the names of towns, countries, etc., when they are without an article.

LXVI. Zu is used instead of the genitive in order to express not that an object belongs to a thing, but that a feeling or action tends towards an object.[39] In this sense, *to* is also rendered by zu.

LXVII. The other prepositions substituted for *of* are the same as are required by the verbs from which the substantives are derived. Thus,—

    to hope for something auf etwas hoffen
    to be afraid of something sich vor etwas fürchten
    something to be wanting an etwas mangeln
    to thirst or hunger for something nach etwas dursten oder hungern
    to strive for something nach etwas streben
    to mock at something über etwas spotten
    to be disgusted at something sich vor etwas ekeln

LXVIII. Verbs like machen, ernennen (to appoint), werben, etc., implying a change in a person or thing, require the substantive expressive of the change to be preceded by zu.

LXIX. Fuß foot, Bogen sheet, Buch quire, Ries ream, Pfund pound, Paar pair, Dutzend dozen, Mal time (the French *fois*), and other names of size, weight, or measure, usually take no plural after numbers.

---

[39] Notice also that the participle present after *of* is turned into an infinitive preceded by zu.

LXX. Names of towns and countries remain usually undeclined, when preceded by an article or pronoun.

LXXI. Scheu comes from scheuen to recoil from, to shy, shun.

Sucht, related to Seuche pestilence and *sick*, signifies a strong propensity, and often enters into compound substantives, which again furnish adjectives and adverbs.

Die Eifersucht jealousy; eifersüchtig jealous.

Die Gewinnsucht the love of gain; gewinnsüchtig greedy of gain.

Die Habsucht covetousness; habsüchtig covetous.

Die Gelbsucht jaundice (a propensity to yellowness); gelbsüchtig jaundiced.

Die Schwindsucht consumption (propensity to waste away); schwindsüchtig consumptive.

Die Zanksucht quarrelsomeness; zanksüchtig quarrelsome.

LXXII. Weise way (wise, guise), manner, is often joined to adjectives (sometimes in the form of a compound) to make adverbs, corresponding with the English adverbial affix *ly*.

"Of" rendered by Prepositions (continued).

of what were they talking (what were they talking of)? von was sprachen sie?	which of them would you recommend? welchen von ihnen würden Sie empfehlen?
of what does this work treat? von was (or wovon) handelt dieses Werk[40]?	I cannot recommend one of them ich kann nicht einen einzigen von ihnen empfehlen
the Lay of the Bell is a celebrated poem by Schiller das Lied von der Glocke ist ein berühmtes Gedicht von Schiller	are you a connoisseur of watches? verstehen Sie sich auf Taschenuhren?

---

[40] *Action*, deed, or a literary work. In the sense of *labour*, work is rendered by die Arbeit. In the sense of *mechanism*, by Uhrwerk, Mühlwerk, etc.

after he was honourably acquitted of the unjust accusation, he took a solemn leave of his friends, and left his ungrateful country for ever nachdem er von der ungerechten Beschuldigung ehrenvoll freigesprochen war, nahm er feierlich Abschied von seinen Freunden, und verließ sein undankbares Vaterland auf immer

you boast of deeds of which you have no great reason to be proud Sie brüsten sich auf Thaten, auf welche (or worauf) Sie keine große Ursache haben, stolz zu seyn

I should like to know, what this youngster is so jealous of ich möchte (gerne) wissen, auf was (or worauf) dieser junge Mensch so eifersüchtig ist

she lay long ill of a fever, but died at last of apoplexy sie lag lange am Fieber krank, starb aber zuletzt an einem Schlagflusse (or am Schlage)

I suffer of the gout ich leide an der Gicht

this is enough to make one die of ennui dieß ist genug, um einen aus (or vor) Langeweile sterben zu machen

do not remind me of his treachery, I think enough of it as it is erinnern Sie mich nicht an seine Verrätherei; ich denke so genug daran

of what metals does this bell consist? aus was für Metallen besteht diese Glocke?

the company was composed of Chinese and Afghans die Gesellschaft bestand aus Chinesen und Afghanen

do you understand, what is to become of the undertaking? sehen Sie ein, was aus dem Unternehmen werden soll?

beware of flatterers hüten Sie sich vor Schmeichlern

what are you afraid of? vor was fürchten Sie sich?

I am not afraid of him; but I am afraid to do a thing of which I should have to be ashamed ich fürchte mich nicht vor ihm; aber ich fürchte etwas zu thun, dessen ich mich schämen müßte

he was ashamed of those who had allowed him nearly to starve er schämte sich vor denen, die ihn hatten beinahe vor Hunger sterben (or umkommen) lassen what does this gentleman complain of? über was (or worüber) beklagt sich dieser Herr?

he complains about the bad accommodation of the hotel er beklagt sich über die schlechte Bedienung des Gasthofes (or in dem Gasthofe)

you are making game of me Sie machen sich über mich lustig

if I did make game of you, you would have a right to complain of (about) me wenn ich mich über Sie lustig machte, so würden Sie ein Recht haben, sich über mich zu beklagen

"To" rendered by Prepositions.

address the parcel to your father-in-law, and my agent shall convey it to him addressiren (or richten, or überschreiben) Sie das Packet an Ihren Schwiegervater, und mein Agent soll es an ihn besorgen

when you come to the gate, fasten your horse to a ring in the wall wenn Sie an das Thor kommen, so binden Sie Ihr Pferd an einen Ring in der Mauer an

the inundation extended to the ramparts; I could therefore carry the provisions only as far as the draw-bridge die Ueberschwemmung erstreckte sich bis an die Wälle; deßhalb konnte ich die Lebensmittel nur bis an die Aufzieh-Brücke bringen[41]

I attached myself to their party, and accompanied them as far as the river ich schloß mich an ihre Gesellschaft an, und begleitete sie bis an den Fluß

an order is gone forth to the police, to prevent all foreigners from writing to their friends abroad es ist ein Befehl an die Polizei ergangen, alle Ausländer zu verhindern, an ihre Freunde im Auslande (or in der Fremde) zu schreiben

I have to put a question to you: are you now really accustomed to these practices? ich habe eine Frage an Sie zu thun: sind Sie nun wirklich an diese Gebräuche gewöhnt?

---

[41] *Bringen* signifies both *to bring* and *to take*.

I applied to his guardian, and handed to him my account id) wandte mich an feinen Vormund, und überreichte ihm meine Rechnung

the fortress will be given up to the besiegers at break of day die Festung wird bei Tagesanbruch an die Belagerer übergeben werden

did not your garden formerly adjoin the town-meadow? stieß nicht Ihr Garten ehemals an die Stadtwiese?

he is justly attached to a prince who has done nothing but good to him er hangt mit Recht an einem Fürsten, der (or welcher) nichts als Gutes an ihm gethan hat

the evil which we do to our fellow-men does but too often come home to us das Böse, das (or welches) wir an* unsern Nebenmenschen verüben, fällt nur zu oft auf uns selbst zurück

one gets accustomed to every thing man gewöhnt sich an alles

attend to my words and answer me to (or upon) what I am going to ask you achten (or merken) Sie auf meine Worte, und antworten Sie mir auf (das) was ich Sie fragen werde

if you will listen to my proposal, you will not put off the meeting to so distant a day wenn Sie auf meinen Vorschlag hören wollen, so werden Sie die Zusammenkunft⁴² nicht auf einen so entfernten Tag verschieben

he puts me off to next year, expecting that in the mean time my claim upon him will be transferred to another er vertröstet⁴³ mich auf's künftige Jahr, in der Erwartung, daß in der Zwischenzeit (or inzwischen, or unterdessen) mein Anspruch werde auf einen andern übertragen werden

---

* An, which in all the former verbs governs the accusative, in the three last instances governs the dative.

⁴² If *meeting* implies a few persons coming together by appointment it is rendered as above; if by accident, by das Zusammentreffen; if it means *assembly*, die Versammlung.

⁴³ *To put off* (a thing) verschieben; (a person) vertrösten.

shall you answer (to) the enquiry which I read to you this morning from the "Times"? werden Sie auf die Nachfrage antworten, die (or welche) ich Ihnen diesen Morgen aus den Times vorlas?

all your rights and privileges will pass over (be transferred) to your heir alle Ihre Rechte und Vorrechte werden auf Ihren Erben übergehen

he will lose all these however, if he goes over to the adverse party er verliert jedoch (or aber) alle diese, wenn er zur Gegenpartei übergeht

can you introduce me to the family? können Sie mich bei der Familie einführen?

I shall always be grateful to you, if you can manage that I may speak to the father this very day ich werde immer dankbar gegen Sie seyn (or ich werde Ihnen immer dankbar seyn), wenn Sie es einrichten können, daß ich den Vater noch heute spreche

why do you so anxiously wish to speak to that gentleman? warum sind Sie so begierig, mit [44] jenem Herrn zu sprechen?

he is on the point of marrying his only daughter to a man who is unworthy of her er ist (or steht) im Begriff, seine einzige Tochter an einen (or mit einem) Mann zu verheirathen, der ihrer unwürdig ist

you think[45] so, because you compare him to yourself Sie glauben das (or Sie sind dieser Meinung), weil Sie ihn mit sich selbst vergleichen

I would not advise you to such a proceeding ich möchte Ihnen nicht zu einem solchen Verfahren rathen

I do not mean to compel you to an enterprise to which your own interest ought to impel you ich denke Sie nicht zu einem Unternehmen zu zwingen, zu welchem (or wozu) Ihr eigener Vortheil Sie antreiben sollte

---

[44] We may also use here the accusative without a preposition diesen Herrn zu sprechen.

[45] *To think*, in the sense of *believe*, is rendered by glauben; otherwise by denken, which is also used for to mean, when it signifies to intend.

you are right; nor am I in the least inclined to it Sie haben Recht; auch bin ich nicht im mindesten dazu geneigt

I urged them to insist on their right; but not to bring the matter to a law-suit ich drang in sie, auf ihr Recht zu bestehen (or zu beharren), aber nicht die Sache zu einem Prozeß (or Rechtshandel) zu bringen

he invites all foreigners to his house er ladet alle Ausländer zu sich ein

if you will come to us to dinner, I will send immediately to our friend, the doctor, and ask him also to dine with us wenn Sie zum Mittagessen zu uns kommen wollen, so will ich gleich[46] zu unserm Freund, dem Doctor, schicken (or senden), und ihn bitten lassen, auch mit (or bei) uns zu speisen

this young officer belongs to a regiment of our garrison dieser junge Offizier gehört zu einem Regiment unserer Garnison

I have sent Mr. N. to you, and sent you at the same time a ream of paper and a bundle of pens ich habe Herrn N. zu Ihnen geschickt, und zugleich schickte ich Ihnen ein Ries Papier und ein Bund Federn

if you have to send anything to your brother-in-law, I shall add several things[47] to your parcel wenn Sie etwas an Ihren Schwager zu senden haben, so werde ich verschiedene Sachen zu Ihrem Packet hinzufügen

does that lady in black belong to your party gehört jene Dame im schwarzen Kleide (or jene schwarzgekleidete Dame) zu Ihrer Gesellschaft?

does that horse belong to you? gehört jenes Pferd Ihnen?

no, it belongs to that gentleman with the great-coat nein, es gehört jenem Herrn mit dem Oberrocke

you speak in relation to things which I do not understand Sie sprechen in Bezug auf Dinge, die ich nicht verstehe

---

[46] Gleich referring to space, means *level, equal*; if referring to time, when it is also called sogleich *immediately*. Zugleich is *at the same time*.

[47] *Thing*, in the most general sense, is das Ding; but if it represents an object at the disposal of man, or which may be thought to be so, it is rendered by die Sache.

what you say, refers to other times than ours was Sie sagen, bezieht sich auf andere Zeiten, als die unserigen   from regard to your opinion, I will be silent aus Achtung vor Ihrer Meinung, will ich schweigen

LXXIII. *To be going, to be about*, if expressive of an immediate future, is usually rendered by the future, ich werde, etc. Otherwise it is by im Begriffe seyn (or stehen), followed by an infinitive with zu, or by wollen, followed by an infinitive without zu.

LXXIV. Verbs expressive of acts done in the presence of others, whether for their imitation or not, are accompanied by vor; as, ich lese ihm vor I read to him; er schreibt dem Kinde vor, und es schreibt ihm nach he writes (makes a copy) for the child, and it writes after him; spielen Sie mir dieses Stück vor, wenn ich es spielen soll play this piece for me (or first), if I am to play it. But vorschreiben is also to dictate, i. e. to order. Hence die Vorschrift the copy (a writing to be copied) and the order, rule of conduct (laid down for us). The copy, that which is written *from* something, is die Abschrift, from abschreiben to copy.

LXXV. Instead of zu meinem, deinem, seinem Hause, etc., we say zu mir, zu dir, zu ihm, etc. At my house in meinem Hause; but also bei mir, bei dir, bei ihm, bei uns, etc.

LXXVI. *To* after schicken, if relating to a person, if the object is also a person, is rendered by zu; if a thing, by an, with the acc., or without a preposition by the dative. If it relates to a place, by nach.

LXXVII. Gehören, signifying *to be owned*, governs the dative; but if *to be connected with*, by zu.

LXXVIII. *Of* between substantives of size, quantity, weight, or measure, and those expressing persons, animals, and things, unless they are preceded by an article, pronoun, or adjective, is not rendered, *the second* noun *being* in the same case as the first. As:

a glass of wine ein Glas Wein
a glass of *the*, of *this*, of *my* wine ein Glas des, dieses, meines Weines
a glass of good wine ein Glas guten Weines

N. B. With an adjective, the word needs not to be in the genitive, we may say, ein Glas guten Wein.

LXXIX. Substantives which in English are preceded by an adjective, are often given in German as compound words, particularly if the previous word should in German be no adjective, or one taken from Latin or French. Thus: the opposite party die Gegenpartei, the same as das Gegengift the antidote, der Gegenkaiser the opposing emperor. Or, die Nationalgarde, die Nationalschuld, der Nationalcharacter the national-guard, debt, character, die Realschule practical school, die Militairschule military school, der Militairdienst military service, die Civilsache civil matter, der Civildienst, der Civilbeamte civil service, civil officer.

DIFFERENT MANNERS OF RENDERING VERBS.

To Be.

1) *Rendered by* seyn.*

I am tall ich bin groß
he is little er ist klein
is she wet? ist sie naß?
is the weather fine? ist das Wetter schön?
it is very fine es ist sehr schön
we are not wet wir sind nicht naß
they are ready sie sind fertig

are you not yet dry? seyd Ihr noch nicht trocken?
was the tailor here to-day? war der Schneider heute hier?
he will be here in an hour er wird in einer Stunde hier seyn
have you been at the post-office? sind Sie auf der Post gewesen?

---

* See also page 12.

no, I have been at the steam-boat office nein, ich bin auf der Dampfschiff-Expedition gewesen

who is it? wer ist es?

who is the man? wer ist der Mann?

it is I ich bin es

it was either he or they es war entweder er oder sie

it is a great pity es ist jammerschade

it is good being here hier ist gut seyn

it was better being there es war besser dort (or dort war es besser)

it is not all gold which glitters es ist nicht alles Gold, was glänzt

there has been a stranger up stairs es ist ein Fremder oben gewesen

we had not been long below wir waren nicht lange unten gewesen

are there any good books to be had in this library? sind gute Bücher in dieser Bibliothek zu haben?

you are now to speak es ist nun an Ihnen zu reden

whose turn is it? an wem ist die Reihe?

is it not my turn? ist die Reihe nicht an mir?

he is as much like his brother as can be er ist seinem Bruder so ähnlich, wie Ein Ei dem andern (as one egg to another)

were I to write to him schriebe ich an ihn

were I to talk to you till doomsday, you would not believe me wenn ich auch bis zum jüngsten Tag zu (or mit) Ihnen redete, so würden Sie mir doch nicht [glauben

be it so es sey

be it so, or not dem sey so, oder nicht

be it, as it may dem sey wie ihm wolle

however this may have been wie dem auch gewesen seyn mag

be he rich or poor sey er (nun) reich oder arm

be it right or wrong mag es nun recht oder unrecht seyn

2) *Rendered by* es giebt, *when it implies general existence.*

what is there to be seen in this town? was giebt es in dieser Stadt zu sehen?

is there a theatre here? giebt es ein Theater hier?

DIFFERENT MANNERS OF RENDERING TO BE. 75

there are many curiosities here es giebt hier viele Merkwürdigkeiten⁴⁸

there are many foreigners among us es giebt viele Ausländer unter uns

there were formerly but very few es gab (deren) ehemals sehr wenige

there will be more of them every year es wird deren alle Jahre mehr geben

there have been better times es hat bessere Zeiten gegeben

what news is there? was giebt's neues?

there is no news in the papers es giebt nichts neues in den Zeitungen

what is the matter? was giebt's?

there is nothing the matter es ist nichts

are there good tailors here? giebt es gute Schneider hier?

there is one in this street who, I am sure, would satisfy you es giebt einen (or es ist einer) in dieser Straße, mit dem Sie gewiß zufrieden seyn würden

3) Rendered by sich befinden.

there are no contraband goods in this trunk es befinden sich keine verbotenen Waaren in diesem Koffer (or dieser Kiste)

how are you (do you do)? wie befinden Sie sich?

how is Her Majesty? wie befindet sich Ihre Majestät?

are your children better? befinden sich Ihre Kinder besser?

they are rather better this moment sie befinden sich diesen Augenblick etwas besser

they were very bad a few days ago sie befanden sich vor ein paar Tagen sehr schlecht (schlimm)

were there no Englishmen in their company? befanden sich keine Engländer in ihrer Gesellschaft?

---

⁴⁸ Literally *markworthinesses*. Curiosity (desire of knowledge) is die Wißbegierde; (eagerness for news) die Neugierde. Curious wißbegierig, neugierig, (remarkable, singular) merkwürdig, eigenthümlich, sonderbar.

4) *Rendered by* gehen *or* stehen.

how is it with him now? wie geht es ihm jetzt? or wie steht es jetzt mit ihm?

thus it is with them so steht es mit ihnen

how is it with her law-suit? wie steht es mit ihrem (or um ihren) Proceß (or Rechtshandel)?

it is (lies) with you to accept the proposal es steht bei Ihnen, den Vorschlag anzunehmen

the matters are as I told you die Sachen stehen, wie ich Ihnen gesagt habe

how is their business? wie steht es mit ihrem Geschäft?

it was very bad with the nation at the close of the last war es stand sehr schlecht mit der (or um die) Nation am Schlusse des letzten Krieges

her life was at stake es ging ihr ums Leben

it was not in my power to do more for them than I had done es stand nicht in meiner Macht, mehr für sie zu thun, als ich gethan hatte

5) *Rendered by* sich lassen, *followed by an infinitive present.*

there is no getting over that dagegen läßt sich nichts einwenden

such a thing may be listened to (or there is something in that) das läßt sich hören

that is not to be done das läßt sich nicht thun

this was to be expected das ließ sich erwarten

how was this to be imagined? wie ließ sich dieß denken?

6) *Rendered by* sollen; *also followed by an infinitive present.*

"Hamlet" was to have been played this evening es sollte diesen Abend „Hamlet" aufgeführt werden

a bridge was to be thrown across the river es sollte eine Brücke über den Fluß geschlagen werden my luggage is to be here this very week mein Gepäck soll diese Woche noch hier seyn

when is Her Majesty to be in town again? wann soll I. M. (Ihre Majestät) wieder in der Stadt seyn?

I am to do it ich soll es thun

if you were to have bought a hat wenn Sie hätten einen Hut kaufen sollen

if so be that he were to leave town this month wenn er ja noch diesen Monat abreisen sollte

7) *Rendered by* wollen.

if one were to believe him wenn man ihm glauben wollte

I was to buy some prints ich wollte (sollte) einige Kupferstiche kaufen

if they were to pay all his debts, they would become poor themselves wenn sie alle seine Schulden bezahlen wollten, so würden sie selbst arm werden

8) *Rendered by* müssen.

if it is to be, who is to prevent it? wenn es seyn (geschehen) muß, wer soll es verhindern?

what is to be, must be was seyn muß, muß seyn

it was all to turn out as it had been foretold es mußte sich alles fügen, wie man es vorhergesagt hatte

there is to be at last an end of his opposition sein Widerstand muß zuletzt ein Ende nehmen

so things were to come so mußten die Sachen kommen

what am I to answer, if he were to ask me? was muß ich antworten, wenn er mich fragen sollte?

9) *In the sense of* "*to concern*" *by* angehen.

what is that to me or to her? was geht das mich oder sie an?

it would have been nothing to you es würde Sie nichts angegangen haben

it is nothing to any one es geht keinen (et)was an

it was something to us all es ging uns alle an

10) *"To be sure"*, *rendered by* ja.

be sure to be in time! kommen (gehen) Sie ja nur zeitig genug!

let him be sure to menti name to him! daß er meinen Namen erwähne!

11) *"To be said, or reported" by* heißen.

it is said es heißt

it is reported man sagt (or erzählt sich)

that is to say das heißt (abbreviated, i. e. d. h.)

that would be saying a gre das hieße viel gesagt

that was not saying mu hieße nicht viel

12) *To be at a loss:*

I am at a loss about it ich kann mich nicht darein finden

if you are at a loss about the matter, I can help you out,

wenn Sie die Sache ni sehen können, so ka Ihnen heraus helfen

13) *Rendered by* haben:

you are right and she is wrong, Sie haben recht und sie hat unrecht

they would be wrong, Sie unrecht haben

he is always right er hat imn

14) *The infinitive past to be rendered by the infinitive present a verb "To be":*

such paper is to be had here solches Papier ist hier zu haben

that is not to be done das läßt sich nicht thun

such a change is to be wis eine solche Veränderung wünschen

15) To BE *rendered by* werben; *in the passive voice.**

I am heard by him ich werbe von ihm gehört

she is not seen by you sie wird nicht von Ihnen gesehen

they are repelled by force sie werden mit Gewalt zurückgedrängt

I was cured by these pills ich wurde durch diese Pillen hergestellt

we were referred to a physician wir wurden an einen Arzt gewiesen

there was much talking es wurde viel gesprochen

there has been no singing es ist nicht gesungen worden (or man hat nicht gesungen)

the courier has been intercepted by the enemy der Courier (Eilbot(h)e) ist vom Feinde aufgefangen worden

the messengers have been detained by the weather die Bot(h)en sind durch das Wetter aufgehalten worden

we had been hindered in our walk wir waren an unserm Spaziergang verhindert worden

let them be esteemed werden sie geachtet

a house was building (being built) in the suburb ein Haus wurde in der Vorstadt gebauet

the cloth way laying (being laid) der Tisch wurde gedeckt

your dinner is getting ready Ihr Essen wird eben zurecht gemacht

your horses are feeding Ihre Pferde werden (eben) gefüttert— or: man füttert (eben) Ihre Pferde

the horses are (just) putting to the carriage die Pferde werden (so eben) angespannt — or: es wird (so eben) angespannt—or: man spannt (so eben) an

16) To BE *before the participle present omitted.**

is he not coming? kömmt er nicht?
are they writing? schreiben sie?

we were enjoying the fine evening wir genoßen den schönen Abend

---

* See also page 35 and remarks XXIX, XXX, page 37.
* See Rem. VII. page 5.

have we not been expecting a letter? haben wir nicht einen Brief erwartet?

had they not been reading the newspapers? hatten Sie nicht die Zeitungen gelesen?

we shall be sailing till dinnertime wir werden bis zur Eßzeit segeln

I would not have been building castles in the air. like him, ich würde nicht gleich ihm Schlösser in die Luft gebaut haben

the meat is boiling das Fleisch kocht

the water is simmering das Wasser simmert

the stars are shining die Sterne scheinen (glänzen)

the moon was hiding itself der Mond verbarg sich

the dog will be barking der Hund wird bellen

the door would have been creaking die Thüre würde geknarrt haben

17) *"There is, there was,"* etc., *variously rendered; frequently through* man:

there was no getting through the gate es war unmöglich durch das Thor zu kommen—or: man konnte nicht durch das Thor kommen

there is excellent soap selling at the shop opposite. man verkauft vortreffliche Seife im Laden gegenüber

there were several new churches building man bauete mehrere neue Kirchen

there will be a ship launched tomorrow man wird morgen ein Schiff vom Stapel lassen

there is no saying, what may happen niemand weiß zu sagen, was sich ereignen könnte

18) *"To be for", and other idiomatic uses of "To be."*

whom are you for? mit wem halten Sie es?

I am for the duke ich halte es mit dem Herzoge—or, ich bin für den Herzog

what are you for? womit halten Sie es? — or was ist Ihre Meinung (Ihr Wunsch)?

DIFFERENT MANNERS OF RENDERING TO BE. 81

I am for any thing you may propose ich bin mit allem zufrieden, was Sie immer vorschlagen mögen

he was absolutely for his son's going to college er bestand durchaus darauf, daß sein Sohn auf die Universität gehen sollte

the young man did it at last, because his mother was also for it der junge Mensch that es zuletzt, weil seine Mutter ebenfalls dafür war (or es ebenfalls wünschte)

he was a father to him er benahm sich wie ein Vater gegen ihn

he is for a good glass of wine and a merry company, seine Sache ist ein gutes Gläschen Wein und eine lustige Gesellschaft

one person is for port, another for sherry, a third for hock, a fourth for champagne, a fifth for burgundy, and a sixth even for malmsey einer trinkt gern (or verlangt, or will) Oporto=, ein anderer Xerres=, ein dritter Rheinwein, ein vierter Champagner,* ein fünfter Burgunder und ein sechster sogar Malvasier

I for my part am for any wine; if it be but pure and good ich meinestheils (or für meinen Theil) bin mit jedem Wein zufrieden (or mir ist jeder Wein recht), wenn er nur rein und gut ist

I am for going immediately ich halte dafür (or fürs beste), daß wir sogleich gehen

he was absolutely for her returning er war durchaus dafür, daß sie zurückkehren sollte

they were for staying sie waren dafür (or sie wollten), daß man bliebe

are you for a water-party, or a trip on land? wollen Sie lieber zu Wasser oder zu Lande gehen?

the Turks are for a speedy administration of justice die Türken lieben eine schnelle Rechtspflege

there, I am rather for France da lobe ich mir doch Frankreich

had it not been for you wenn es nicht Ihnen zu Gefallen geschehen wäre — or, wären Sie nicht gewesen

that will be the death of me das bringt mich um (or um's Leben)

---

* Pronounce Shampanyer

G

To Have

1) *In the sense of " to hold" or " possess," and as an auxiliary to active verbs, is rendered by* haben.

where have you my cloak? wo haben Sie meinen Mantel?

my servant has it mein Bedienter hat ihn

he has had it just now er hat ihn so eben gehabt

have your sisters got my drawings? haben Ihre Fräulein Schwestern meine Zeichnungen?

no, sir, I have them in my travelling-bag nein, mein Herr, ich habe sie in meinem Reisesack (or Nachtsack)

2) *As an auxiliary to neuter verbs, by* seyn.*

we have been on the continent wir sind auf dem Continent gewesen

in the course of time, the drummer has become a general im Laufe der Zeit ist der Trommelschläger ein General geworden

such things have happened more than once solche Dinge sind mehr als einmal geschehen (or haben sich mehr als einmal ereignet, or zugetragen)

you had not stayed long enough; I wish, you had stayed but one month longer Sie waren nicht lange genug (da) geblieben; ich wollte, Sie wären nur Einen Monat länger geblieben

we were but just arrived in town wir waren nur eben in der Stadt angekommen

they had all gone out sie waren alle hinausgegangen

who has run into the cabin? wer ist in die Kajüte gelaufen?

had not his servant fallen down stairs and broken his arms? war sein Bedienter nicht die Treppe herunter (or hinunter †) gefallen und hatte (sich) den Arm zerbrochen?

he has taken a walk er ist spazieren gegangen

they had taken a ride sie waren spazieren (or aus)geritten

---

* See also p. 10. † See p. 23.

DIFFERENT MANNERS OF RENDERING TO HAVE.

I shall have taken a drive, before he is gone there ich werde spazieren (or aus)gefahren seyn, ehe er hingegangen ist

I should have driven into the country ich würde aufs Land gefahren seyn

the groom would have leapt over the gate⁴⁹ der Reitknecht würde über das Gatter gesprungen seyn (or gesetzt⁵⁰ haben)

the trees have budded die Bäume sind ausgeschlagen

the cats would have crept in at the window die Katzen würden zum Fenster hineingekrochen seyn

you had fallen into bad company Sie waren in schlechte Gesellschaft gerathen

the child is fallen asleep das Kind ist eingeschlafen

it would have awoke by the noise es würde durch den Lärm aufgewacht seyn

where have you met them? wo sind Sie ihnen begegnet?

3) *In the sense of "to cause," by* laffen.*

I am having a coat made of your tailor ich lasse mir einen Rock bei Ihrem Schneider machen

had she not a dress made of my dress-maker? ließ sie sich nicht ein Kleid bei meiner Schneiderinn machen?

we have had our port-manteau repaired wir haben unsern Koffer ausbessern lassen

had they not their port-manteaus brought in doors? hatten sie nicht ihre Koffer in's Haus bringen lassen?

they will have the room shown to them sie werden sich das Zimmer zeigen lassen

by whom have you had this book printed bei wem⁵¹ haben Sie dieses Buch drucken lassen?

---

⁴⁹ Gate (of a house or town) das Thor; (of a garden) die Thüre; (of a parc field, etc.) das Gatter.

⁵⁰ To leap (in person) springen; with a horse (setzen).

* See Note ¹⁴, p. 25.

⁵¹ Bei wem corresponds with the French chez qui — at whose house?

have you not these books from Paris? haben Sie diese Bücher nicht von Paris kommen laſſen?

the duchess of —— has all her fur from St. Petersburgh die Herzoginn von —— läßt all ihr Pelzwerk von St. (Sanct) Petersburg kommen

have a physician, if you feel unwell laſſen Sie einen Arzt rufen, wenn Sie ſich unwohl fühlen

I was lately obliged to have one in the middle of the night ich mußte neulich einen mitten in der Nacht kommen laſſen

we have all our vegetables and butter direct from our farm wir laſſen all unſer Gemüſe und unſere Butter von unſerm (Meier)-hofe (or Vorwerk) kommen (or wir bekommen all u. ſ. w.[52])

have me excused laſſen Sie mich entſchuldigen

4) *In the sense of "to wish" or "require," by* wollen, wünſchen, verlangen, mögen, *or by* ſollen *or* müſſen.

I will not have you write to him ich will nicht haben, daß Sie an ihn ſchreiben

he would not have her ride out this evening er wünſchte (mochte) nicht, daß ſie heute Abend ausritte

I would not have you for any thing in the world sign this paper ich möchte um alles in der Welt nicht, daß Sie dieſes Papier unterſchrieben

God will have us love our neighbour Gott will, daß wir unſern Nächſten lieben

will you have me address myself to the minister? wollen Sie, daß ich mich an den Miniſter wende (or wenden ſoll)?

what would you have? was wollen Sie?

what will he have me to do? was will er, daß ich thun ſoll? (or was ſoll ich machen (or thun)?

if you will have me attend, you must speak seriously wenn ich aufmerkſam ſeyn ſoll, ſo müſſen Sie ernſthaft ſprechen

I would have you know Sie müſſen wiſſen

---

[52] Und ſo weiter, etc.

I will do any thing you would have me ich will alles thun, was Sie verlangen

I had rather have one cup of tea than two cups of coffee ich wollte lieber eine Tasse Thee, als zwei Tassen Kaffee haben

he had rather stay at home er möchte lieber zu Hause bleiben

I had rather see him than let him go away disappointed es ist besser ich sehe ihn, als daß er mit getäuschter Erwartung weggehe

5) *In the sense of " to buy" by* kaufen:

you have that horse too dear Sie haben jenes Pferd zu theuer gekauft

6) *To " let have" by* zukommen lassen *or* verkaufen:

he let me have the watch for ten guineas er ließ mir die (Taschen) uhr für zehn Guineen zukommen — or, er verkaufte mir die Uhr für 10 Guineen

let me have your snuff-box, lassen Sie mir Ihre (Schnupftabacks) dose zukommen (or verkaufen Sie mir Ihre Dose)

7) *" To have" in the sense of " to assert" by* behaupten.

my father will have it that my brother is not gone to India mein Vater behauptet, mein Bruder sey nicht nach Indien gegangen

people will have it so man behauptet es

8) *In the sense of " to possess," by* besitzen.

he has the art of making himself friends every where, er besitzt die Kunst sich allenthalben Freunde zu machen (or erwerben)

she had the art of pleasing, and she made the best use of it sie besaß die Kunst zu gefallen, und machte den besten Gebrauch davon

9) *" In the sense of " to advise," by* rathen.

I would have you return him the money ich rathe Ihnen ihm das Geld zurückzugeben

he will not do as I would have him er will meinen Rath nicht or, er will mir nicht folgen.

I would not have you send it back to him by any means ich rathe Ihnen, es durchaus nicht zurückzuschicken or ich bin ganz und gar nicht der Meinung, daß Sie es ihm zurückschicken

you won't do as I would have sie wollen nicht thun wie ich Ihnen rathe, or sie wollen meinem Rathe nicht folgen

10) *Idiomatic phrases with to have.*

he has his lesson by heart er kann (weiß) seine Aufgabe auswendig

have a care nehmen Sie sich in Acht or, hüten Sie sich

let him have his desert man behandle ihn, wie er es verdient

have him away führen (schaffen) Sie ihn fort

I was obliged to have her up stairs ich mußte sie heraufkommen lassen

she had like to have fallen into a swoon sie wäre beinahe in Ohnmacht gefallen (gesunken)

have them in lassen Sie sie herein kommen

the ship had like to have sunk das Schiff wäre beinahe zu Grunde gegangen or, es hätte nicht viel gefehlt, so wäre das Schiff versunken

it must be had, cost what it will es muß geschafft werden (or, wir müssen es haben), es koste, was es wolle.

this must be had in your remembrance Sie müssen dieses nie aus den Gedanken lassen

as fortune would have it zu allem (or, zum) Glücke

To Become.

1) werden.

he has become my most faithful friend er ist mein treuester Freund geworden

this will come to nothing daraus *wird nichts*

what is become *of* him? was ist aus ihm geworden?

he became at last very rich er wurde zuletzt sehr reich

2) geziemen, sich schicken, zukommen.

it becomes a man of honour to speak the truth es geziemt einem Manne (or es schickt sich für einen Mann) von Ehre, die Wahrheit zu sprechen

do what becomes a man of honour to do, thun Sie was einem (ehrlichen) rechtschaffenen Manne zu thun zukömmt

3) gut stehen, gut lassen.

this bonnet becomes you exceedingly well dieser Hut stehet (läßt) Ihnen vortrefflich

every thing becomes handsome people schönen Menschen stehet (läßt) alles gut

4) *To become acquainted with* lernen, kennen lernen.

I fear, I shall never become thouroughly acquainted with this language ich fürchte, ich werde diese Sprache nie vollkommen lernen

where did you become first acquainted with Mr. N. — ? wo haben Sie (den) Herrn N.— zuerst kennen lernen?

I became acquainted with him on my voyage to South-Australia ich lernte ihn auf meiner Reise nach Süd-Australien kennen

you will become acquainted with a first rate man Sie werden einen tüchtigen Mann kennen lernen

To BE ABLE können, vermögen, im Stande seyn.

we are not able (or cannot) see in the dark im Dunkeln kann man nicht sehen

the blind can see nothing at all die Blinden können gar nicht sehen — or vermögen gar nicht zu sehen

without spectacles I am not able to read ohne Brille kann ich nicht lesen — or, bin ich nicht im Stande (or vermag ich nicht) zu lesen what can you do! was können Sie thun!

I can read and write ich kann schreiben und lesen

my brother can read Italian mein Bruder kann Italienisch lesen

we can read to each other wir können einander vorlesen

I was to write, but I could not ich sollte schreiben, aber ich konnte nicht

he was to speak French, but he was not able er sollte Französisch sprechen, aber er vermochte es nicht

why were they not able to make themselves understood? warum konnten Sie sich nicht verständlich machen?

I can see the light, but he can not ich kann das Licht sehen, er aber (kann) nicht

can you see it indeed? können Sie es wirklich sehen

I could see it half an hour ago ich konnte es vor einer halben Stunde sehen

he could not (was not able) to go out er konnte nicht ausgehen or: vermochte nicht auszugehen

she has not been able to bear the light sie hat das Licht nicht ertragen können — or: zu ertragen vermocht

why has she not been able? warum hat sie es nicht gekonnt — or: vermocht?

the horses have not been able to draw this heavy carriage die Pferde haben diesen schweren Wagen nicht ziehen können — or: zu ziehen vermocht or sind nicht im Stande gewesen, den schweren Wagen zu ziehen

he had not been able to leave town before er hatte die Stadt nicht zuvor verlassen können — or: zu verlassen vermocht — or: er ist nicht im Stande gewesen die Stadt zuvor (or früher) zu lassen

shall you be able to answer his letter by to-day's post? werden Sie seinen Brief mit der heutigen Post beantworten können — or zu beantworten vermögen — or zu beantworten im Stande seyn

I have not been able to find a private lodging in the whole town ich habe in der ganzen Stadt keine Privatwohnung finden können (or zu finden vermocht)

he has not been able to walk five miles in an hour er hat nicht fünf Meilen in Einer Stunde gehen können (or zu gehen vermocht), (or er ist nicht im Stande gewesen, fünf Meilen u. s. w. zu gehen)

I should like to have such a parrot, if I could have it ich hätte gern einen solchen Papagei, wenn ich ihn haben könnte

it is as bad as it can es kann nicht schlimmer seyn

we should not have been able to dispatch the parcel so soon wir würden nicht haben das Packet so bald abschicken können (or wir würden nicht das Packet so bald abzuschicken vermocht haben, or nicht im Stande gewesen seyn, das Packet so bald abzuschicken)

it rained as fast as it could es regnete, was es konnte (or was das Zeug hielt)

run as fast as you can laufen Sie, was Sie laufen können

"CAN" *rendered by* wissen.

how can you tell that? wie (or woher) wissen Sie das?

this is more than I can tell ich weiß nichts davon

nobody could tell es wußte niemand etwas davon

can you tell, how it will turn out? wissen Sie, wie es ablaufen wird?

TO LIKE, TO BE INCLINED, TO CHUSE, TO WISH (WANT, DESIRE), MAY, MIGHT.

a) *Rendered by* mögen.

we did not like to inform him of his loss wir mochten ihm nicht gern seinen Verlust bekannt machen

she did not want any more tea sie mochte keinen Thee mehr

do you like pine-apples? mögen Sie Ananas?

I like them very well, but they do not like me; that is, they don't agree with me ich mag sie wohl, aber sie mögen mich nicht; das heißt, sie bekommen mir nicht (or sie vertragen sich nicht mit mir, or ich kann sie nicht vertragen)

he prefers beer to wine er mag lieber Bier als Wein

do you like her cousins? mögen Sie ihre Cousinen?

I like the eldest very well; but I abominate the others ich mag die älteste wohl, aber ich verabscheue die andern

one ought to abominate no one man sollte niemanden verabscheuen

you may say what you like; but these pert young persons with their sharp eyes and yet sharper tongues could drive one mad Sie mögen sagen, was Sie wollen, aber diese vorlauten jungen Personen mit ihren stechenden Augen und noch stechenderen (or schärferen) Zungen möchten einen zum Wahnsinn treiben (or toll machen)

that is the reason why I do not choose to go to your friend's parties das ist die Ursache, weßwegen ich nicht zu Ihrer Freundinn Gesellschaften gehen mag

I did not choose to sell my horse ich mochte mein Pferd nicht verkaufen

he may dine whenever he pleases er mag zu Mittag essen, wann es *ihm beliebt*

it threatened to rain; yet they did not like to take an umbrella with them es drohte zu regnen; dennoch mochten sie keinen Regenschirm mitnehmen

I did my best to persuade them to it; now they may for my part get wet ich that mein möglichstes, sie dazu zu bereden; nun mögen sie meinethalben naß werden

how could you wish such a thing? wie mochten Sie so etwas wünschen?

may you never experience the effects of his bad conduct! mögen Sie nie die Folgen seiner schlechten Aufführung erfahren!

would you not wish to be in my place? möchten Sie nicht an meiner Stelle seyn?

I should like it, if it were possible ich möchte es wohl, wenn es möglich wäre

that may have happened once or twice das mag ein- oder zweimal geschehen seyn

now that I have heard of him, they may say what they please jetzt, da ich von ihm gehört habe, mögen sie sagen, was sie wollen

DIFFERENT MANNERS OF RENDERING MAY.

you may go to the East or West Indies Sie mögen nach Ost- oder Westindien gehen

I should like to be at home now ich möchte jetzt zu Hause seyn

b) "MAY" rendered by können.

it may yet snow before night es kann noch vor Nacht schneien

what reward may they expect? was für eine Belohnung können sie erwarten?

you may now hear it confirmed Sie können es jetzt bestätigt hören

it may be es kann seyn

as for me you may do it, or let it alone meinethalben können Sie es thun oder bleiben lassen

I should like to have such a canary-bird, if I might ich möchte gern einen solchen Kanarienvogel haben, wenn ich könnte (or dürfte)

c) "MAY" rendered by dürfen.

I should like to buy this inkstand, but I may (must) not ich möchte wohl dieses Dintenfaß kaufen, aber ich darf nicht

why may you not? warum dürfen Sie nicht?

I may not spend so much money without my tutor's leave ich darf, ohne meines Hofmeisters Erlaubniß, nicht so viel Geld ausgeben

when we had a holyday, we might play at whatever game we pleased wann wir einen Spieltag hatten, so durften wir spielen, was wir wollten

may I read this letter? darf ich diesen Brief lesen?

may I take the liberty to ask you a question? darf ich so frei seyn, eine Frage an Sie zu thun?

may I offer you a wing of this chicken? darf ich Ihnen einen Flügel von diesem Hühnchen anbieten?

you may depend upon me, if on no one else Sie dürfen sich auf mich verlassen, wenn Sie sich auf niemand anders verlassen dürfen

I thought, it might be true ich dachte, es dürfte wahr seyn

you might engage in the business, but not a youth of his age Sie durften sich mit dem Geschäft befassen, aber nicht ein Jüngling seines Alters

if I might, I would not hesitate a moment wenn ich dürfte, so würde (or wollte) ich nicht einen Augenblick anstehen

To be obliged (must).

a) *Rendered by* müssen.

must he say it? muß er es sagen?

you must not, if you do not wish it Sie müssen nicht, wenn Sie nicht wollen

we were obliged to get up before day-light wir mußten vor Tage aufstehen

what were you obliged to pay for the *visa* of your pass-port? was mußten Sie für die Visirung (or Unterzeichnung) Ihres Passes bezahlen?

if I must, I will wenn ich muß, so will ich

b) Must *rendered by* dürfen.

you must not converse with people of this description Sie dürfen (or müssen) mit Leuten dieses Schlages sich nicht unterhalten

I must not take this medicine tonight ich darf diese Medizin heute Abend nicht nehmen

Shall, should, ought, to be (*followed by an infinitive*), to let, *rendered by* sollen.

who shall go in first? wer soll zuerst hineingehen?

you shall Sie sollen es

you shall address the stranger in German Sie sollen den Fremden auf Deutsch (or in der deutschen Sprache) anreden

let them take care of themselves (or beware) sie sollen sich in Acht nehmen

you ought to prepare at once for your journey Sie sollten sich sogleich für (or auf) Ihre Reise vorbereiten that shall be a warning to me das soll mir eine Warnung seyn

that should not happen again das sollte nicht wieder geschehen

to whom ought he to address himself under these circumstances? an wen sollte er sich unter diesen Umständen wenden?

if I am to be the spokesman, you must tell me what I am to say wenn ich der Redner seyn soll, so müssen Sie mich belehren, was ich sagen muß (or soll, or zu sagen habe)

who is to bell the cat? wer soll der Katze die Schelle anhängen?

at what o'clock were we to be at the ambassador's? um wie viel Uhr sollten wir bei dem Gesandten seyn?

we were to be there at half past 4 precisely wir sollten präcis (genau) um halb fünf da seyn

they were to come to an agreement before his Excellency's departure sie sollten vor der Abreise Seiner Excellenz eine Uebereinkunft treffen

To WILL, BE WILLING, WANT, ETC., BY wollen.

I will, if I can ich will, wenn ich kann

he will, if he may er will, wenn er darf

we accompany you, because we chuse to do so wir begleiten Sie, weil wir es wollen

will you not accompany them all? wollen Sie sie nicht alle begleiten?

he sent for me, but I would not come er ließ mich rufen, aber ich wollte nicht kommen

she too preferred to stay in her room auch sie wollte lieber in ihrem Zimmer bleiben (or sie zog es vor, in Ihrem Zimmer zu bleiben)

we were just going to refuse their request wir wollten ihnen eben ihr Gesuch abschlagen

they wanted to have their names included in the list of subscribers sie wollten ihre Namen in die Subcriptionsliste eingeschlossen haben (or wissen)

weak characters *wish*; only the strong *will* schwache Naturen wünschen; nur die starken wollen

but after all it is only God who enables us both to will and to do am Ende jedoch ist es nur Gott, der uns in den Stand setzt, sowohl zu wollen, als zu vollbringen

MISCELLANEOUS SENTENCES ON THE VERBS können, mögen, dürfen, müssen, sollen, wollen, ESPECIALLY IN THE PERFECT, PLUPERFECT, FUTURE, AND CONDITIONAL TENSES.

he has been obliged to rest several times er hat sich mehrere Male ausruhen müssen

we have been obliged to discharge our man-servant at a moment's notice wir haben unsern Bedienten auf der Stelle verabschieden müssen

I have not been permitted to have any intercourse with my relations ich habe keinen Umgang mit meinen Verwandten haben dürfen

I was therefore obliged to reside at an inn ich habe deßhalb in einem Gasthafe logiren (wohnen) müssen

I am to have a coat from my tailor in an hour's time ich soll binnen einer Stunde einen Rock von meinem Schneider haben (or empfangen)

you were to have had your new boots yesterday morning Sie hatten Ihre neuen Stiefeln gestern morgen haben sollen

if he had been willing to send them in time, I could have recommended him to my partner wenn er sie hätte zu rechter Zeit schicken wollen, so hätte ich ihn meinem Associé* empfehlen können

I would have accompanied them, if I had been able ich würde sie begleitet haben, wenn ich gekonnt hätte

you ought to have kept all the presents that were sent you Sie hätten alle die Geschenke behalten sollen, die Ihnen geschickt wurden

I might have done so, if I had wished it ich hätte es thun können, wenn ich (es) gewollt hätte

your attorney was to have drawn up the agreement between them, but he said that he dared not do it Ihr Anwalt hatte den Vertrag zwischen ihnen ausfertigen sollen, aber er sagte, er dürfe es nicht (thun)

---

* A partner in commerce; also Theilhaber, Genoß — (at play) Mitspieler— (in dancing) Tänzer, Tänzerinn —(husband) Gatte (wife) Gattinn.

but I imagine, he would not have been able, even if he had been permitted aber mich däucht, er würde nicht gekonnt haben, selbst wenn er gedurft hätte

he has re-paid no more than he has been obliged er hat nicht mehr zurückbezahlt, als er gemußt hat (or als er hat bezahlen müssen)

I shall not be able to reach town so soon ich werde die Stadt nicht sobald erreichen können

he will be obliged to sell his railway-shares er wird seine Eisenbahn-aktien verkaufen müssen

she will not be allowed either to write or to receive letters sie wird weder Briefe schreiben, noch empfangen dürfen

they will be required to subscribe a declaration of confidence in the new administration sie werden eine Erklärung unterschreiben sollen, daß sie in die neue Verwaltung Vertrauen setzen

the guardian will not feel inclined to let his ward act according to his own pleasure der Vormund wird den Mündel nicht gern nach eigenem Gutdünken gewähren lassen mögen

they will not be inclined to accept our invitation sie werden unsere Einladung nicht annehmen wollen

they will be expected to communicate their secret to the government sie werden ihr Geheimniß der Regierung mittheilen sollen

might I have kept the whole? hätte ich das Ganze behalten können?

you would have been obliged to consult a physician Sie würden haben einen Arzt um Rath fragen müssen

the physicians would have wished to hold a consultation die Aerzte würden haben eine Consultation (or Berathung) halten wollen

he would willingly have restored the patient, if he had been able er würde den Kranken gern wieder hergestellt haben, wenn er gekonnt hätte

if he had been inclined, he could have done much towards the improvement of the people wenn er gemocht (or gewollt) hätte, so hätte er viel für die Verbesserung des Volkes thun können he would not be allowed to marry so young, even if he wished it er würde nicht so jung heirathen dürfen, selbst wenn er es wollte

you would needs have to go and see what is the matter Sie würden nothwendiger Weise gehen und sehen müssen, was es gi(e)bt

he would not have been obliged to leave his bride immediately after the ceremony, if he had not had to meet his steward in the country on some very important business er würde nicht genöthigt gewesen seyn, seine junge Gemahlinn gleich nach der Trauung zu verlassen, wenn er nicht hätte seinen Verwalter, einer wichtigen Angelegenheit wegen, auf dem Lande treffen müssen

I shall have to oppose him at the next election ich werde ihm bei der nächsten (Parlaments)wahl entgegentreten müssen

I would accompany you to the opera, if I might ich würde Sie nach der Oper begleiten, wenn ich dürfte

he could not get on er konnte nicht weiter

he would not have been able to get on er würde nicht weiter gekonnt haben

they will not have been able to perform the "Wallenstein" with so small a company sie werden mit einer so kleinen Truppe nicht haben den „Wallenstein" aufführen können (or sie werden nicht im Stande gewesen seyn, mit einer so kleinen Truppe den „Wallenstein" aufzuführen)

I shall be expected to wait on the minister, whether I like it or not ich werde dem Minister aufwarten (or meine Aufwartung machen) sollen, gleichviel ob ich es mag oder nicht

I cannot help blaming you ich kann nicht umhin, Sie zu tadeln

I cannot but laugh, when I hear you talk in this strain ich muß lachen, wenn ich Sie auf diese Weise reden höre

make all the haste you can eilen Sie, so viel Sie können

let him come back as soon as he can lassen Sie ihn sobald wie möglich wieder (or zurück)kommen

as sure as can be ganz gewiß

that is the safest course that can be dies ist das allersicherste Mittel

If I may say so wenn ich so sagen darf

I should feel myself happy, if I might devote my life to so useful an undertaking ich würde mich glücklich schätzen, wenn ich mein Leben einem so nützlichen Unternehmen weihen (or widmen) dürfte (or könnte)

may it please Your Majesty Ihre Majestät geruhen

there shall be nothing wanting es soll an nichts fehlen

you ought not to have doubted his word Sie hätten sein Wort nicht bezweifeln sollen

you shall certainly not be wronged es soll Ihnen gewiß kein Unrecht geschehen

I should not wonder, if he were to buy this bad copy for a real Titian es sollte mich nicht wundern, wenn er diese schlechte Copie für einen ächten Titian kaufte

LXXX. The verbs können, müssen, sollen, mögen, dürfen, wollen, having in German infinitives and participles, form all their tenses like other verbs. The corresponding English verbs, being defective, form many of their tenses by paraphrases; whence the difficulty of translating them into German.

LXXXI. There is a peculiarity in them in German, that when their past participles govern an infinitive, the participle is usually turned into an infinitive itself, which is also the case with lassen, hören, sehen, lehren, lernen, and helfen.

LXXXII. Können expresses physical power.

Mögen, a moral power, or the absence of a prohibition, besides liking and possibility.

Dürfen, a permission, and sometimes a daring; also a possibility, especially in the imperfect subjunctive.

Sollen, a moral obligation, generally rendered in English by *to be*. It is also rendered by *to be said*.

Müssen, a physical or moral necessity (what we *ought* may be resisted, but not what we *must*).

Wollen, a volition.

H

N.B. When *shall* and *will*, *should* and *would* are used in their primary signification, they must be respectively rendered by follen or wollen; otherwise they are the signs of the future or conditional.

LXXXIII. Möchte emphatically expresses, like the French *voudrais*, a wish, and is generally accompanied by the adverb gern, and the comparative is lieber, of which the superlative am liebsten.

LXXXIV. When *may* and *might* are employed as signs of the subjunctive mood, they are not rendered by a separate word, but the verb itself is put in the subjunctive.

LXXXV. The subjunctive in the regular verb differs from the indicative only in the third person of the present, which ends in e instead of t. In irregular verbs the present subjunctive is always regular; and the imperfect subjunctive differs from the imperfect indicative by taking e in the first and third person singular when the latter is without it, and by changing the a, o, or u, of the latter into ä, ö, or ü.

To LET (*permit, allow*), TO LEAVE, TO CAUSE (*make, have*) laffen.

let the birds fly laffen Sie die Vögel fliegen

who has let the dog out of the room? wer hat den Hund aus dem Zimmer hinausgelaffen?

we let them bawl as much as they liked wir ließen sie schreien, so viel sie wollten

why have you not let them enquire after their school-fellow? warum haben Sie sie nicht nach ihrem Schulkameraden (ihrer Mitschülerinn) fragen laffen?

if you will leave your things in this room, they will be quite safe wenn Sie Ihre Sachen in diesem Zimmer laffen wollen, werden sie ganz sicher (or verwahrt) seyn

where have you left your repeater? wo haben Sie Ihre Repetieruhr gelaffen?

you may do it, or leave it alone Sie mögen es thun, oder bleiben laffen well, then I shall leave it alone nun, so werde ich es bleiben lassen

let me see: if I leave him alone with this little pickle, he is sure to let him do any mischief he likes lassen Sie mich sehen: wenn ich ihn mit diesem kleinen Wildfang allein lasse, so läßt er ihn gewiß alles Unheil anrichten, das er nur immer mag (wozu er nur immer Lust haben mag)

let me go lassen Sie mich fort

are you not having something new made? lassen Sie sich nichts Neues machen?

I am having a German manuscript translated by him ich lasse ihn eine deutsche Handschrift (or handschriftliche Arbeit) für mich übersetzen

he caused all his prisoners to be executed er ließ alle seine Gefangenen hinrichten

if he had not had them executed, they would have risen against his own troops wenn er sie nicht hätte hinrichten lassen, so würden sie sich gegen seine eigenen Truppen erhoben haben (or würden sie gegen seine ...... aufgestanden seyn)

where do they intend to have the bridge thrown across the river? wo denken sie die Brücke über den Fluß schlagen zu lassen?

why don't you let your servant pack up your clothes? warum lassen Sie nicht Ihren Bedienten Ihre Kleider einpacken?

when I lately had my carriage sold, your son-in-law was just having one built als ich neulich meinen Wagen verkaufen ließ, ließ Ihr Schwiegersohn sich eben einen bauen

I must have all my linen washed, before I continue my journey ich muß alle meine Sachen (Wäsche) waschen lassen, ehe ich meine Reise fortsetze

if I have not enough linen, I must send for some more from home wenn ich nicht Wäsche genug habe, muß ich mir noch welche von Hause kommen lassen

would it not be more advisable to let your valet fetch it würde es nicht rathsamer seyn, sie von Ihrem Kammerdiener holen zu lassen?

no, it will be quite as safe, to have it sent by railway nein, es wird eben so sicher seyn, sie auf der Eisenbahn schicken zu lassen

if you are not better to-morrow morning, I advise you, to send for a physician or a surgeon wenn Sie sich morgen früh nicht beſſer befinden, ſo rathe ich Ihnen, einen Arzt oder Wundarzt kommen zu laſſen.*

"To LET" as *Imperative*.

let us put an end to the matter laſſen Sie uns (or wir wollen) der Sache ein Ende machen (or machen wir der Sache ein Ende)

let him learn his lesson laſſen Sie ihn ſeine Aufgabe lernen (or er lerne ſeine Aufgabe)

let them earn their own living laſſen Sie ſie (or ſie mögen) ihr Brod ſelbſt verdienen

let them learn patience lernen Sie ſie Geduld haben (or laſſen Sie ſie Geduld lernen)

let us depart gehen wir (or laſſen Sie uns gehen, or wir wollen fort)

now let us run as fast as we can jetzt laſſen Sie uns laufen (or laufen wir), was wir können (or was das Zeug hält)

MISCELLANEOUS SENTENCES ON THE FOREGOING VERBS.

you shall do it this very moment Sie ſollen es dieſen Augenblick thun

I will do it, if I can ich will es thun, wenn ich kann

no one does, what he should niemand thut, was er ſollte

I would perform all my duties, if I were not too weak ich würde alle meine Pflichten erfüllen, wenn ich nicht zu ſchwach wäre

will you confide it to me? wollen Sie es mir anvertrauen?

I shall do it with pleasure ich werde es mit Vergnügen thun

what will he (does he want) of me? was will er von mir?

---

* See also Note ¹⁴, page 25.

he will not be inclined to tell it you now es wird es Ihnen jetzt nicht sagen wollen

he would not, but was obliged er wollte nicht, aber er mußte

I have not been willing, although I ought ich habe nicht gewollt, obgleich ich gesollt hätte

I shall order him, but he will not be willing to obey me ich werde es ihm befehlen, aber er wird mir nicht gehorchen wollen

I offered him my assistance, but he would not have it ich bot ihm meine Hülfe an, aber er hat sie nicht gewollt

you will then have received your dictionary Sie werden alsdann Ihr Wörterbuch empfangen haben

he would confide in you, if he knew you, as I do er würde sich Ihnen anvertrauen, wenn er Sie kennte, wie ich (Sie kenne)

at times he will know me; but at others he will pass me, as if I were a perfect stranger to him zuweilen kennt er mich; aber zu andern Zeiten geht er an mir vorüber, als wenn er gar nichts von mir wüßte

to his superiors he will bow and scrape, but to his inferiors he will be as rude as possible gegen seine Vorgesetzten weiß er sich zu bücken und zu schmiegen, aber gegen seine Untergebenen kann er so grob seyn wie einer

the mad-man would at one time take himself for an elephant, and at another for a tea-pot der Verrückte hielt sich bald für einen Elephanten, bald für eine Theekanne

on such occasions, he would smile bei solchen Gelegenheiten pflegte er zu lächeln

if pressed, they would acknowledge that they had wronged us wenn man in sie drang, gestanden sie wohl, daß sie uns Unrecht gethan hätten

you are to do me a great favour Sie sollen mir eine große Gefälligkeit erzeigen

I will, if it is in my power recht gern, wenn es in meiner Macht steht

I wish, you would give me a letter of introduction to Mr. N. at Geneva ich wollte, Sie gäben mir einen Empfehlungsbrief an Herrn N. zu Genf

I know the gentleman very well, and an introduction to him

might be of service to you; but I had rather, you got one from some one else ich kenne den Herrn recht gut, und eine Empfehlung an ihn könnte (or dürfte) Ihnen von Nutzen seyn; aber ich möchte lieber, Sie ließen sich eine von irgend jemand anderm geben

he is not the man of whom I would like to ask a favour, or to be beholden to er ist nicht der Mann, von dem ich eine Gefälligkeit verlangen, oder dem ich mich für verpflichtet halten möchte

such a question is not to be decided in a moment solch eine Frage läßt sich nicht in einem Augenblicke entscheiden

these complicated affairs were not to be settled in one day diese verwickelten Angelegenheiten ließen sich nicht in Einem Tage abmachen

arguments like these were cogent enough Gründe wie diese ließen sich (wohl) anhören

if it is feasible, it shall be done wenn es sich ausführen (or thun) läßt, soll es geschehen

nothing else was to be expected *es ließ sich nichts andres erwarten*

whether he be right or wrong, I can no more interfere in their quarrels er mag (nun) Recht haben oder nicht, ich kann mich nicht mehr in ihre Streitigkeiten mischen

he says, happen what will, he had washed his hands of the whole business er sagt, es geschehe was da wolle, so wolle er nichts mehr mit der ganzen Sache zu schaffen haben

I doubt, whether anything more agreeable could have happened ich zweifle, ob irgend etwas Angenehmeres sich hätte ereignen können

if I knew what I had to answer, I should not mind meeting the great man and hearing what he has to ask wenn ich wüßte, was ich antworten müßte, so würde ich mir nichts daraus machen, dem großen Mann entgegenzutreten, und zu hören, was er zu fragen hat

If one always could as one might wish, one might pass through life very easily wenn man immer könnte, wie man wollte (or gern möchte), so dürfte man sehr leicht das Leben durchschreiten

I should be sorry, if I always could what I would. Man but too often desires that which he ought not es sollte mir leid thun, wenn ich immer könnte, was ich wollte. Der Mensch will nur zu oft das, was er nicht sollte,

might I ask you for your vote at the approaching election? dürfte ich Sie um Ihre Stimme bei der bevorstehenden Wahl bitten?

happen what will, our friend is sure of his re-election es komme (or geschehe, or ereigne sich), was da wolle, so ist unser Freund gewiß, wieder gewählt zu werden

be that, as it may dem sey, wie ihm wolle

may it be a black horse, or must it be a grey? darf es ein Rappe, oder muß es ein Schimmel seyn?

the colour of the horse may be what it will die Farbe des Pferdes darf (or mag) seyn, welche sie wolle

LXXXVI. *Will* and *would*, signifying "to be accustomed," are rendered by pflegen, or are altogether passed over, or just indicated by the addition of wohl to the verb they accompany. See Examples p. 101.— *Would*, expressive of desire, is rendered by möchte.

TO BE CALLED, TO ORDER OR BID, TO BE SAID (*reported*) heißen.*

what have you bidden him to translate was haben Sie ihn übersetzen heißen?

who has ordered you to learn so many pages by heart? wer hat Sie so viele Seiten auswendig lernen heißen?

I bade them to enter into the dining-room ich hieß sie in den Speisesaal (or das Speisezimmer) treten

that is what I call making a good bargain das heiße ich gut einkaufen

---

* See p. 14 and p. 78.

To see sehen, to hear hören, to teach lehren, to learn lernen, to help helfen.*

see, what he is reading sehen Sie, was er liest

I have not seen him read ich habe ihn nicht lesen sehen

have you ever heard her recite? haben Sie sie je declamiren hören?

I have heard her once, when I was lately in town ich habe sie einmal gehört, als ich neulich in der Stadt war

what are you teaching him? was lehren Sie ihn?

I am teaching him to speak German ich lehre ihn Deutsch sprechen

I thought you had taught him to speak this language long ago ich dachte, Sie hätten ihn diese Sprache schon längst sprechen lehren (or gelehrt)

I am having this plough-boy learn both to write and read ich lasse diesen Bauernburschen so wohl schreiben als lesen lernen

where have you become acquainted with him? wo haben Sie ihn kennen lernen?

I became acquainted with him during my residence at my neighbour's country-house ich lernte ihn während meines Aufenthaltes in meines Nachbars Landhause kennen

during this disastrous campaign we have learnt to deny ourselves während dieses unglücklichen Feldzuges haben wir entbehren lernen

help me out of this difficulty helfen Sie mir aus dieser Schwierigkeit

no one else has been able to help me out of it niemand anders hat mir daraus helfen können

his pretended friends have helped him to squander the money which his father had scraped together seine angeblichen Freunde haben ihm das Geld verschwenden helfen, welches sein Vater zusammengescharrt hatte

I cannot help it ich kann nichts dafür (or ich kann es nicht ändern, or verhindern)

---

† See Remark LXXXI, p. 97.

all I did was of no use alles, was ich that, half nichts

of what use would a knowledge of all the languages of Europe be to any one in the East-Indies? was würde eine Kenntniß aller Sprachen Europas einem in Ostindien helfen?

however much I must blame his misconduct, I cannot help pitying his misfortune so sehr ich auch sein Mißverhalten tadeln muß, so kann ich doch nicht umhin, sein Unglück zu bedauern

pray, help yourself bedienen Sie sich doch selbst

will you help your neighbour to some of this calf's head? wollen Sie Ihrem Nachbar (or Ihrer Nachbarinn) etwas von diesem Kalbskopf vorlegen?

you help no one at table Sie bedienen niemanden bei Tische

if I could have helped it, my cousin would never have engaged in any business with him wenn ich es hätte verhindern können, so würde mein Vetter sich nie mit ihm in ein Geschäft eingelassen haben

I did what I could not help ich that, was ich nicht lassen konnte

To amuse.

amuse yourself, as well as you can vertreiben Sie sich die Zeit, so gut Sie können

we amused them by telling them long stories [54] about elfs and fairies wir unterhielten sie durch die Erzählung langer Mährchen von Elfen und Feen

he amuses himself with his curiosities er vergnügt sich mit seinen Seltenheiten

we looked for something solid, but were amused with fair words wir erwarteten etwas Solides (or Handgreifliches), aber wurden mit schönen Worten hingehalten

To answer.

what have you to answer to this? was haben Sie hierauf zu antworten?

how will you answer his question? wie wollen Sie seine Frage beantworten?

---

[54] Mährchen, fairy-tales; Geschichten or Erzählungen, stories or tales of real or possible events.

that does not answer das paßt (or taugt) nicht

what do you think will answer your purpose best? was, denken Sie, wird Ihrer Absicht am besten entsprechen?

if your scheme answers, I have no objection wenn Ihr Plan gut ausfällt, so habe ich nichts dagegen

I shall know how to answer for myself ich werde mich (schon) selbst zu vertheidigen wissen

your expectation will never be answered Ihre Erwartung wird nie erfüllt werden

he was to answer for the event with his head er sollte mit seinem Kopfe für den Ausgang (gut)stehen

I make you answerable for the consequences before God and the world ich mache Sie vor Gott und der Welt für die Folgen verantwortlich

such a responsibility I cannot take upon myself eine solche Verantwortlichkeit kann ich nicht auf mich nehmen

could you answer it to your own conscience? konnten Sie es gegen Ihr eigenes Gewissen verantworten?

that will never answer a good end das fällt gewiß nicht gut aus (or das läuft gewiß nicht gut ab)

mine host, no one answers a bell or a call in your house Herr Wirth, man mag in Ihrem Hause klingeln (or schelten) oder rufen so viel man will, es läßt sich niemand sehen

you have been answered; now get home as fast as you can Sie haben Ihre Antwort, machen Sie sich nun nach Hause so schnell Sie können

if any one were to ask me, what answer should I give him? wenn mich jemand fragen sollte, was sollte ich ihm zur Antwort (or zum Bescheid) geben?

ask something of him, and you will hear from his answer, whether he likes to give fordern (or verlangen[55]) Sie etwas von ihm, und Sie werden aus seiner Antwort hören, ob er gern giebt

---

[55] *Notice*, that to ask a question is fragen, and to require any thing is fordern or verlangen.

has any one answered the door? ist jemand nach der Hausthüre gegangen (or hat jemand die Hausthüre geöffnet)?

LXXXVII. Many verbs requiring prepositions after them (like antworten), renounce these for the accusative case (like beantworten), when they have assumed the prefix be. As, ich trat in das Zimmer, or betrat das Zimmer.

To apply.

he has applied from childhood to drawing and painting; indeed, his application has been quite proverbial er hat sich von Jugend auf auf das Zeichnen und Malen gelegt; ja, sein Fleiß ist zum Sprüchwort geworden

how do you propose to apply your time during the holydays? wie meinen Sie während der Ferienzeit (or Vacanz) Ihre Zeit zu verwenden?

he applied all his care, talent, skill and leisure to the education of his children er wandte alle seine Sorgfalt, sein Talent, seine Geschicklichkeit und seine Muße auf die Erziehung seiner Kinder

apply nothing to your wound but bread and water poultice legen Sie nichts auf Ihre Wunde, als nur einen Aufschlag von Brod und Wasser

many men have foolishly applied their fortune to the maintenance of the drama or opera viele haben thörichter Weise ihr Vermögen an die Aufrechthaltung des Dramas oder der Oper gewandt

no one likes to apply an offensive parable to himself niemand wendet gern eine beleidigende (or anstößige) Parabel auf sich an

to whom could I apply in such an emergency if not to a friend? an wen könnte ich mich in einer solchen Noth wenden, wenn ich mich nicht an einen Freund wenden darf?

if you will apply (or address yourself) to the ministry, you must do it in writing wenn Sie sich an's Ministerium wenden wollen, so müssen Sie es schriftlich thun

LXXXVIII. *To like* is most frequently rendered by the verb implied in English, such as *to have, to eat, to drink, to walk, to sleep, to see, to hear*, etc., with the adverb gern (see Rem. LXXXIII, p. 98). Thus:—

do you like those people, and do you like to be in their company? haben Sie diese Leute gern und sind Sie gern in ihrer Gesellschaft?

few people like to live (or are fond of living) by themselves wenige Menschen leben (or wohnen) gern allein

do you like cheese after your dinner? essen Sie gern Käse nach Tische?

yes, and I like a glass of good beer with it ja, und ich trinke gern dabei ein Glas gutes Bier

did he not prefer the Flemish school of painting to any of the Italian? hatte er nicht die niederländische Malerschule lieber, als irgend eine von den italienischen?

what she likes best is a ball and supper was sie am liebsten hat, ist ein Ball und Nachtessen

I am glad to hear that you are fond of German music es ist mir lieb zu wissen (or zu erfahren), daß Sie deutsche Musik gern haben (or hören)

To appoint, appointment; disappoint.

the duke appointed him his private secretary der Herzog ernannte ihn zu seinem Privatsekretär

we have appointed four o'clock to meet at my hotel wir haben mit einander ausgemacht (or wir sind übereingekommen), daß wir *einander* um vier Uhr in meinem Gasthofe treffen sollen

what hour has he appointed for you to call on him? welche Stunde hat er Ihnen bestimmt zu ihm zu kommen?

I shall take care to be there even before the appointed time ich werde es mir zur Pflicht machen, selbst vor der bestimmten Frist dort zu seyn it is not right to disappoint any one, least of all when you have made an appointment with a person es ist nicht recht, irgend jemanden (in seiner Erwartung) zu täuschen (or jemanden vergeblich warten zu lassen), am wenigsten, wenn man einem zugesagt hat

he expected an appointment under the new governor general; but met with disappointment er erwartete eine Stelle (or ein Amt) unter dem neuen Generalgouverneur zu erhalten; hat sich aber getäuscht gefunden

why can you not come at the time the general appointed you? warum können Sie nicht zur Zeit kommen, die der General Ihnen bestimmt (or anberaumt) hat?

because I have already an appointment for it weil ich schon zur selben Zeit versagt bin

which day is appointed for the wedding? welcher Tag ist für die Hochzeit angesetzt (or anberaumt, or bestimmt)? (or welchen Tag soll die Hochzeit statt finden)

To bear.

each man had to bear (carry) not only his musket and accoutrements, but also six days' provision jeder Soldat hatte nicht nur seine Flinte und Gepäck, sondern auch Lebensmittel auf sechs Tage zu tragen

the king bore a sceptre in one hand and a globe[56] in the other der König trug ein Scepter in einer und einen Reichsapfel in der andern

we ought to bear each other's burdens wir sollten einer des andern Bürden tragen

if his favourite son does not bear off the prize at the next examination, he will be very much disappointed wenn sein Sohn beim nächsten Examen nicht den Preis davonträgt, wird er sich sehr gekränkt fühlen

---

[56] The common word for globe is die Erdkugel or merely Kugel. The heavenly globes die Himmelskörper.

women in general bear bodily pain better than men die Weiber ertragen körperliche Schmerzen gewöhnlich besser als die Männer

I will bear half the expence ich nehme die Hälfte der Kosten auf mich

bear with us a little longer haben Sie noch etwas Geduld mit uns

will your assertion bear being examined into? wird Ihre Behauptung eine Untersuchung aushalten können?

the British cavalry at Waterloo bore down every thing before them by the weight of their horses die englische Reiterei warf bei Waterloo mittelst der Schwere ihrer Pferde alles vor sich nieder

after having bombarded Copenhagen, Nelson bore off the whole of the Danish fleet nachdem er Copenhagen beschossen hatte, nahm Nelson die ganze dänische Flotte mit fort

there are difficulties in my undertaking, I know; but I know too what will bear me out ich weiß, daß mein Unternehmen seine Schwierigkeiten hat; aber ich weiß auch, was mich hindurchführen (or mir durchhelfen) wird

people who have to live with spoiled children have much to bear with wer mit verzogenen Kindern zusammen leben muß, hat viel zu dulden

I wonder, whether he expects that I shall bear him out this time too ich möchte wissen, ob er erwartet, daß ich ihn auch diesmal vertheidige (or daß ich ... seine Sache führen solle)

the result has borne me out that I was right der Erfolg hat bewiesen, daß ich Recht hatte

you must bear up against misfortune Sie müssen sich im Unglück zu fassen wissen

what reputation does he bear among his countrymen? in was für einem Ruf steht er bei seinen Landsleuten?

he bears me a grudge, I believe ich glaube, er grollt mir

she bears a great resemblance to her grandmother sie ist ihrer Großmutter sehr ähnlich

the strange sail bore right upon us das unbekannte Schiff kam gerade auf uns los gesegelt

the fleet bears too much to the East die Flotte steuert zu sehr ostwärts

LXXXIX. After kommen, gehen, laufen, and similar verbs, the past participle is often used without its being wanted in English, or when it is represented by a participle present.

Being (*participle and substantive*).

much that we regard as evil, is far from being so in reality vieles, das der Mensch als ein Uebel betrachtet (or für ein Uebel hält), ist wirklich keines

his being at last gone ought rather to rejoice than to grieve you daß er endlich fort (or gestorben) ist, sollte Sie eher freuen als betrüben

who will attempt to fathom the being of God, if our own remains a mystery to us! wer will es wagen, das Wesen Gottes erforschen zu wollen, da uns unser eigenes ein Geheimniß bleibt!

to whom else do we owe our being but to Him? wem anders als ihm haben wir unser Daseyn zu verdanken?

can there be a human being who really does not believe in the existence of a Supreme Being? kann es ein menschliches Wesen geben, das wirklich nicht an das Daseyn eines höchsten Wesens glaubt?

in Him we live and move and have our being in ihm leben, weben und sind wir

being ashamed to meet his rival after he had refused his challenge, he went a great way round to avoid him da er sich schämte, seinem Nebenbuhler, nachdem er dessen Herausforderung abgelehnt (hatte), unter die Augen zu treten, so ging er einen weiten Weg um (or machte er einen langen Umweg), um ihn zu vermeiden

not being afraid to give offence to any one by her talk, she let her tongue run on without mercy da sie nicht fürchtete, irgend jemanden durch ihr Geschwätz zu beleidigen, ließ sie ihrer Zunge freien Lauf

man, being what he is, must expect changes in life da der Mensch nun einmal so ist, so muß er Veränderungen (or Wechselfälle) in seinem Leben erwarten

To BID.

bid them come in bitten Sie (or ersuchen Sie, or lassen Sie) sie hereinkommen

they bade me to a grand dinner sie luden mich zu einem großen Gelage ein

I am at your bidding ich stehe zu Ihrem Befehle

I have bidden farewell to all such vanities long ago ich habe allen diesen Eitelkeiten schon längst entsagt (or Valet, or Lebewohl gesagt)

do as you are bidden thun Sie, was Ihnen befohlen wird (or man Ihnen befiehlt)

I must now bid you good night ich muß Ihnen jetzt gute Nacht sagen (or wünschen)

bidding me so little for the estate as you do, I can hardly believe that you really think of purchasing it da Sie mir so wenig für das Gut bieten, so kann ich mir kaum denken, daß Sie es im Ernste zu kaufen (or erstehen) meinen

To BLEED.

with a wound still bleeding, he insisted on being bled in the arm bei noch blutender Wunde bestand er darauf, daß man ihm am Arm zur Ader lassen solle

with a bleeding heart he bade his family an eternal farewell mit blutendem Herzen nahm er von seiner Familie für immer Abschied

To BOIL.

see that the beef be well boiled sehen Sie zu, daß das Rindfleisch gut durchgekocht werde

does the water boil? kocht das Wasser?

it is just on the boil es ist so eben am Sieden

do not let the liquid boil over lassen Sie nicht die Flüssigkeit überkochen (or überlaufen)

To break.

whatever will not bend in his hands, must break was sich nicht unter ihm biegen will, muß brechen

falling with his horse, he broke his neck er stürzte mit dem Pferde und brach das Genick

letting glass fall to the ground, it will break wenn Sie Glas zu Boden fallen lassen, so zerbricht es

you rack your brains in vain Sie zerbrechen sich den Kopf umsonst

having broken your word so often, who is to believe you in future? da Sie Ihr Wort so oft gebrochen haben, wer wird Ihnen künftig Glauben schenken?

he who breaks the law is amenable to the law wer das Gesetz verletzt, fällt dem Gesetz anheim

the waves break against the rocks die Wellen brechen sich an den Felsen

I am at a loss how to break the news to her that the marriage of her daughter is broken off ich weiß nicht recht, wie ich ihr die Nachricht beibringen soll, daß die Heirath ihrer Tochter abgebrochen ist

I am afraid it will break the poor old lady's heart ich fürchte, sie werde der armen alten Frau das Herz brechen

he has now broken with all his relations er hat jetzt mit allen seinen Verwandten gebrochen (or sich mit ...... entzweiet)

the thief who lately broke into our house, has now broken prison der Dieb, welcher neulich in unserm Hause einbrach, ist nun aus dem Gefängniß gebrochen

this merchant having lost his fortune by the breaking of our bank, had nothing left to him but to break too da dieser Kaufmann durch den neulichen Bruch unserer Bank sein ganzes Vermögen verloren (or eingebüßt) hatte, so blieb ihm nichts übrig, als selbst zu falliren (or Bankrott zu machen)

it is no easy matter to break oneself of inveterate bad habits es ist nichts Leichtes, sich eingewurzelte Unarten abzugewöhnen

I did not like to leave before the company broke up ich wollte nicht gern weggehen, ehe die Gesellschaft aufbrach (or sich trennte)

the whole of the officers, having been found guilty of cowardice by a court-martial, were broken by an order of the commander-in-chief alle die Offiziere, nachdem ſie von einem Kriegsgericht der Feigheit überwieſen worden, wurden durch einen Befehl des Obergenerals (or Oberbefehlshabers) caſſirt

the whole scheme was broken up by one of those accidents which no prudence can foresee and no skill repair der ganze Plan fiel zu Boden, in Folge von einem jener Zufälle, welche keine Klugheit vorherzuſehen, und keine Geſchicklichkeit gut zu machen vermag

when does your school break up? wann fangen Ihre Ferien an?

the plague which then broke out, prevented the out-break of a revolution, and perhaps of a general war die Peſt, welche alsdann ausbrach, hinderte den Ausbruch einer Revolution, und vielleicht eines allgemeinen Krieges

mind, that that savage dog does not break from his chain ſehen Sie zu, daß jener biſſige Hund ſich nicht von der Kette losreißt

pardon me, if I break in upon your privacy entſchuldigen Sie mich, wenn ich Sie in Ihrer Einſamkeit ſtöre

what is it that thus breaks your rest? was iſt es (wohl), das Sie ſo in Ihrer Ruhe (or Ihrem Schlafe) ſtört?

To CALL.

waiter! will you be so good as to call the chamber-maid Kellner! wollen Sie ſo gut ſeyn, das Stubenmädchen zu rufen

who calls? wer ruft?

1. The lady in number 5 called you ich. Die Dame auf Nummer fünf hat Sie verlangt (or hat nach Ihnen gefragt)

she calls for her linen ſie verlangt ihre Wäſche

even the boys in the street call after him ſelbſt die Gaſſenbuben rufen ihm nach

he called the rogue aside, and then called him by his real name er rief (or nahm) den Schelm auf die Seite, und nannte ihn dann bei ſeinem wahren Namen

that is what I call being punctual
das nenne ich (einmal) pünktlich
seyn

the pope having called a council, the emperor called a diet da der Papst ein Concilium (zusammen) berufen hatte, so schrieb der Kaiser einen Reichstag aus

having been called away, I could not call on you, as I had intended da ich abgerufen wurde, so konnte ich nicht bei Ihnen einsprechen (or Sie nicht besuchen), wie ich die Absicht gehabt hatte

although engaged in a serious business, you allow yourself to be called off by every idler who chances to drop in upon you obgleich mit einer wichtigen Sache (or Angelegenheit) beschäftigt, lassen Sie sich (doch) von jedem Müßiggänger, der gerade zu Ihnen kömmt (or der Sie zufällig besucht), davon abrufen (or abziehen)

you have no right, I believe, to call me to account for what I do or not ich glaube, Sie haben kein Recht, mich wegen meines Thuns und Lassens* zur Rede zu stellen

how do you call this in England?
was nennt man das in England?

being in difficulties, he called his creditors together, and these made him call in his debts da er sich in Schwierigkeiten befand, so rief er seine Gläubiger zusammen, und diese ließen ihn seine Schulden einfordern

these circumstances must call to your mind the things you seem to have forgotten, and recall you to your senses diese Umstände müssen Sie an die Dinge erinnern, die Sie vergessen zu haben scheinen, und Sie wieder zur Vernunft zurückbringen

it is now of no use your calling God to witness of your good intention; you ought to have come, when I called for your assistance es hilft nun nichts, daß Sie Gott zum Zeugen Ihrer guten Absicht anrufen; Sie hätten kommen sollen, als ich Sie zu Hülfe rief

now I shall call him in, and call for his opinion jetzt werde ich ihn hereinrufen (lassen), und ihn auffordern, mir seine Meinung zu sagen

---

* Literally doing and omission.

he has been called to the bar er ist zum Advokaten ernannt worden

call me to-morrow morning at half past six wecken Sie mich morgen früh um halb sieben

at the call of passion the youth starts into manhood beim Ruf der Leidenschaft wird der Jüngling plötzlich zum Manne

if you neglect your calling, how can you expect to prosper? wenn Sie Ihren Beruf vernachlässigen, wie können Sie erwarten, daß es Ihnen gut gehe?

tell my servant to remain within call sagen Sie meinem Bedienten, er solle in der Nähe bleiben

being absent at the call of the muster-roll, he was reported as a deserter da er beim Verlesen nicht zugegen war, so wurde er als Deserteur (or Ausreißer) gemeldet

I should have given you a call long ago, if I had known your present residence ich würde Sie schon längst besucht haben, wenn ich gewußt hätte, wo Sie jetzt wohnen

To care.

caring for all, no one cares for him für alle sorgend, bekümmert sich niemand um ihn

left a helpless widow, all her children were cared for by her friends als hülflose Wittwe hinterlassen, wurden alle ihre Kinder von ihren Freunden versorgt (or untergebracht)

you have no business to care for such a spendthrift Sie brauchen sich um einen solchen Verschwender nicht zu bekümmern

what do I care? was frage ich danach?

she cared for nobody sie kümmerte sich um die ganze Welt nicht (or machte sich aus der ganzen Welt nichts)

he did not care a farthing for his reproaches er scherte sich nicht im geringsten um seine (or dessen) Vorwürfe

if they had cared more for the china I sent you, you would have received it all unbroken wenn man auf das Porzlan, das ich Ihnen schickte, besser Acht gehabt hätte, so würden Sie es unzerbrochen erhalten haben

I do not care a straw (a rush, a pinch of snuff) for it ich kümmere mich den Henker drum (or ich frage nicht einen Pfifferling, or eine Prise Taback) danach

I never cared much for melons ich machte mir niemals viel aus Melonen

you would not care to lose your good name es würde ihnen wohl nicht angenehm (or erfreulich) seyn, wenn Sie Ihren guten Ruf verlören (or einbüßeten)

would you care to go with me this summer to Switzerland? möchten Sie wohl diesen Sommer mit mir nach der Schweiz reisen?

I don't care, if I do es verschlägt mir nichts, wenn ich mit Ihnen gehe

take care, you do not trust him again who has cheated you once hüten Sie sich, daß Sie dem nicht wieder trauen, der Sie einmal betrogen hat

he does not take sufficient care of his health er nimmt seine Gesundheit nicht genug in Acht (or wahrt .... nicht genug)

when you see your friends, you should cast away all your cares wenn Sie mit Ihren Freunden zusammen sind, so sollten Sie sich alle Sorgen aus dem Sinne schlagen

he could not have possibly shown more care for his own affairs than he shewed for ours er hätte kaum für seine eigenen Angelegenheiten mehr Sorgfalt beweisen können, als er für die uns(e)rigen bewies

be careful for nothing sorgen Sie für nichts

if they had been careful, I have no doubt, they would have succeeded in all their plans wenn sie vorsichtig zu Werke gegangen wären, so zweifle ich nicht, daß ihnen alle ihre Pläne gelungen seyn würden

XC. The Participle Present is scarcely ever used in German, except adverbially, such as in the phrase " caring for all," etc., p. 116.

XCI. When it expresses a *cause* or a *concurrent event*, it is turned into the Present, Imperfect or Pluperfect of the Indicative preceded by one of the conjunctions da since, weil because, indem, während whilst, nachdem after, the tense depending on the time stated in the accompanying clause. See p. 120 and 122.

When it is used as a verbal substant. after the prepositions, it is often turned into an infinitive, but often into the indicative preceded by daß, while the prepos. is combined with da. As: I had not the least doubt of their being willing to serve us ich hatte nicht den geringsten Zweifel daran, daß sie bereit seyn würden, uns zu dienen.

XCII. For half past 12 we say halb eins (half one), for half past one halb zwei (half two) and so on. With the minutes beyond the half hour, we also mention the next hour; but do not say, how many minutes are wanting, but how many are gone towards it. As 25 minutes to 3, fünf und dreißig Minuten auf drei; a quarter to 4 drei Viertel auf vier; 5 minutes to 5 fünf und fünfzig Minuten auf fünf.

In other instances *half* halb is *added* to the numbers, which must be *ordinal* and always the *next* to the one mentioned in English. Thus instead

of ein und ein halb   ($1\frac{1}{2}$)   say anderthalb
— zwei und ein halb   ($2\frac{1}{2}$)   — drittehalb
— drei und ein halb   ($3\frac{1}{2}$)   — viertehalb
— zehn und ein halb   ($10\frac{1}{2}$)   — elftehalb
— zwanzig und ein halb ($20\frac{1}{2}$) — ein und zwanzigstehalb

To carry.

let some one carry my luggage on board lassen Sie jemand mein Gepäck an Bord tragen (or bringen)

you surely won't carry this heavy parcel yourself! Sie werden doch diesen schweren Pack nicht selbst tragen wollen!

who will carry the prize this time? wer wird dies Mal den Preis davon tragen?

I never carry gold and silver in the same side of my purse ich führe niemals Gold- und Silbermünze in derselben Seite meiner Börse

he carries a noble heart in his breast er führt ein edles Herz in seiner Brust

one ought not to carry arms for mere show man sollte nicht die Waffen zur bloßen Schau führen

men-of-war have to carry, besides their guns, the necessary complement of sailors, and provisions often for many months, also large bodies of troops with their arms, baggage etc, die Kriegsschiffe müssen nebst ihren Kanonen, ihrer nöthigen Mannschaft und Proviant (or Lebensmittel), oft auf viele Monate, auch starke Abtheilungen Truppen nebst deren Waffen, Gepäck u. s. w. tragen (or führen)

the question is, how to carry off the superabundance of moisture die Frage ist, wie der Ueberfluß an Feuchtigkeit abzuführen sey

many a man travels through the world for his amusement, but is never amused, because he carries his ennui with him in his travelling carriage mancher durchreist die Welt, um sich die Zeit zu vertreiben, findet aber niemals Unterhaltung, indem er die Langeweile in seinem Reisewagen mit sich führt

I pray you, do not carry your obstinacy farther. You might repent it ich bitte Sie, treiben Sie Ihre Hartnäckigkeit (or Ihren Trotz) nicht weiter. Sie dürften es bereuen

better to carry gold in your pockets, than on your coat es ist besser man führt das Gold in der Tasche, als daß man es auf dem Rocke trägt

if we had brought any thing into the world, we should have some reason to expect that me might carry something out of it wenn wir etwas in die Welt mitgebracht hätten, so hätten wir guten Grund zu erwarten, daß wir etwas mit hinaus nehmen würden (or dürften)

let us not allow ourselves to be carried away by the wind of every new doctrine lassen wir uns nicht von dem Winde jeder neuen Lehre fortreißen

such arguments ought to carry conviction into every ingenuous mind solche Gründe sollten jedes aufrichtige Gemüth überzeugen

if you expect to carry every thing before you, you will find yourself mistaken wenn Sie erwarten, alles durchführen zu können, so werden Sie finden, daß Sie sich geirrt haben

with money much may be carried, yet not all mit Geld läßt sich vieles durchsetzen, jedoch nicht alles that would be carrying coals to Newcastle das hieße heißes Wasser warm machen

the Dutch carry on their negotiations like their business, with prudence and moderation die Holländer betreiben ihre Unterhandlungen wie ihre Geschäfte, mit Vorsicht und Mäßigung

he carries his head too high er ist viel zu stolz

I wish you would carry on your dispute with a little less heat ich wollte, Sie setzten Ihren Streit mit etwas weniger Hitze fort

he carries on both shoulders er trägt auf beiden Achseln

To change.

I have changed my opinion of this man ich habe meine Meinung über diesen Mann geändert

having got wet through, you ought as quickly as possible to go home and change your clothes da Sie durchnaß geworden sind, so sollten Sie so schnell wie möglich nach Hause gehen, und die Kleider wechseln

she says, she has changed her mind sie sagt, sie habe sich anders besonnen

she is for ever changing her mind sie verändert immer ihre Ansichten (or Entschlüsse) — sie ist sehr wetterwendisch

she is as changeable as the wind sie verändert sich wie der Wind (or dreht sich mit dem Winde)

where shall we change horses? wo wechseln wir die Pferde?

let us change dictionaries. How much must I give you in exchange? wir wollen unsere Wörterbücher tauschen. Wie viel muß ich Ihnen (im Tausche) herausgeben?

when the moon changes, we may hope that the weather will change too wenn der Mond wechselt, so dürfen wir hoffen, daß das Wetter sich auch verändern werde

why did she change colour, when I spoke of the possibility of her changing her religion? warum veränderte sie die Farbe, als ich von der Möglichkeit sprach, daß sie zu einer andern Confession übergehen könnte?

an Irishman once asserted that he had been charged in his infancy ein Irländer behauptete einmal, er sey in seiner Kindheit untergeschoben (or vertauscht) worden

can you change a ten-pound-note for me? können Sie mir eine zehn Pfund (Bank)note wechseln?

yes, if you will take it all in sovereigns; for I have no small change in the house ja, wenn Sie es ganz in Souverainen nehmen wollen; denn ich habe kein klein Geld im Hause

great changes have taken place in Europe since the end of last war es haben sich seit dem Ende des letzten Krieges große Veränderungen in Europa zugetragen

your grand-father tells me, he has made a considerable change in his will to the benefit of his youngest grand-son Ihr Großvater sagt mir, er habe eine bedeutende Aenderung in seinem Testamente getroffen, und zwar zum Besten seines jüngsten Enkels

a change has come over his spirits sein Sinn hat sich geändert

To charge.

being himself charged with too many cares, he charged his old tutor with the education of his son selbst zu sehr mit Sorgen belastet, übergab er die Erziehung seines Sohnes seinem alten Hofmeister (or Lehrer)

there is no telling with what crimes we may be charged, if we displease our arbitrary ruler es ist unmöglich zu sagen, welche Verbrechen man uns zur Last legen, (or welcher ... man uns beschuldigen) dürfte, wenn wir uns(e)rem gewaltsamen Herrscher mißfallen

there is no knowing with what the vessel may be charged niemand weiß, mit was das Schiff beladen seyn mag

I charge you once for all not to go to that place again ich verbiete Ihnen ein für alle Male wieder an diesen Ort zu gehen

our cavalry charged the enemy most vigorously, and this charge decided the battle in our favour unsere Reiterei fiel wüthend über den Feind her, und dieser Angriff entschied die Schlacht für uns (or zu unserm Vortheil)

the poor family, after having struggled for many years with abject poverty, has at last become chargeable to the parish die arme Familie, nachdem sie Jahre lang gegen die bitterste Armuth angekämpft (hatte), ist endlich dem Kirchspiele zur Last gefallen

is your gun charged? ist Ihre Flinte geladen?

you are, it seems to me, not chargeable with vanity man kann Ihnen, wie mich dünkt, keine Eitelkeit vorwerfen (or zur Last legen)

To come.

how did that come? wie kam das (or wie trug sich das zu?)

come what will es komme, was da wolle

if it should come to the worst, you can come and live with me wenn es am schlimmsten kommen (or ablaufen) sollte, so können Sie bei mir wohnen (or im schlimmsten Falle können Sie u. s. w.)

coming so often to town as you do, why do you never come and see us? da Sie so oft nach der Stadt kommen, warum besuchen Sie uns nie?

how does the boy come on at school? was macht der Knabe für Fortschritte in der Schule?

they came on one by one sie kamen einzeln heran

you will come in for your share Sie werden Ihren Antheil empfangen (or erhalten)

some obstacle must have come in the way of the mail, that it is not come in yet es muß der Post ein Hinderniß in den Weg gekommen seyn, daß sie noch nicht herein ist

I shall come into any thing that may be decided on ich werde in alles willigen (or einstimmen), worüber man einig werden mag

no one could come out of a difficulty with greater glory niemand konnte sich mit mehr Ruhm aus einer Schwierigkeit (or schwierigen Lage) herausziehen

fear came upon the whole assembly die ganze Versammlung wurde von Angst befallen

he expected to come off victorious, but he came off a loser *er erwartete den Sieg davon zu tragen, aber er blieb im Verluste*

they say that by often washing the head, the hair comes off *man sagt, daß wenn man sich öfters den Kopf wäscht, einem die Haare ausfallen*

with this rain and mild weather every thing will come up rapidly *bei diesem Regen und dieser milden Witterung wird alles schnell aufkommen (or wachsen)*

she had fallen into a fainting fit, but after a while she again came to (herself) *sie war in Ohnmacht gefallen (or gesunken), aber nach einer Weile erholte sie sich wieder*

what do you think will our bill come to? *wie hoch meinen Sie, daß unsere Rechnung sich belaufen werde?*

that does not by any means come up to our expectation *das reicht durchaus nicht an unsere Erwartung*

I feel old age gradually coming upon me *ich fühle es, daß ich allmälig älter werde*

this came to pass, while no one dreamt of the most distant danger *dies ereignete sich, da niemand sich im entferntesten etwas von Gefahr träumen ließ*

if he goes on at this rate, he must speedily come to ruin *wenn er auf diesem Wege fortgeht, muß er bald (or muß es bald mit ihm) zu Grunde gehen*

it is true, we came at last to an agreement, but I am sure, I came short by half of what was my due *es kam freilich zuletzt zwischen uns zu einem Vergleich, aber ich bin gewiß, ich kam dabei um die Hälfte von dem zu kurz, was mir gebührte*

first come, first served, is an old proverb *wer zuerst kommt, mahlt erst*, ist ein altes Sprüchwort*

if all comes to all, I still feel that I come short of you in many things *wenn es um und um kömmt, so fühle ich doch, daß ich Ihnen in vielen Dingen nachstehe*

how did the new play come off? *wie lief das neue Stück ab?*

they came off second best *sie zogen den kürzeren*

---

* *Literally*, grinds first.

how much of her god-mother's property will come to the young lady wie viel von ihrer Gevatterinn Vermögen wird dem jungen Frauenzimmer zufallen?

if it comes to that, I shall confess at once, how I came to be acquainted with him, and how I came by the manuscripts wenn es dahin kommen sollte, so werde ich auf einmal (or ohne Anstand) bekennen, wie ich mit ihm bekannt geworden, und wie ich zu den Manuscripten gekommen bin

you may rub till doomsday, the spot won't come out sie mögen bis zum jüngsten Tag reiben, und werden den Flecken doch nicht herausbringen

where did this come from? wo haben Sie dieses her?

I should like to know what will come of such conduct ich möchte wissen, wohin eine solche Aufführung führen wird

they came upon me unawares, while I was in my study sie überfielen mich ganz unerwartet in meinem Studierzimmer

it came upon them like a thunderclap es befiel sie, wie ein Donnerschlag

what has all their cunning come to now? wie weit haben sie es nun mit all ihrer List gebracht?

the whole affair is come to nothing die ganze Sache ist zu nichts geworden

come good, come evil, I shall be at my post es falle aus, wie es wolle, so bin ich an meinem Posten

To Disappoint.

precocious children often disappoint the expectations of their parents frühreife Kinder hintergehen oft die Erwartungen ihrer Eltern

I expect you without fail, and trust, you will not disappoint me again, as you are in the habit of doing ich erwarte Sie ohne Fehl, und hoffe, Sie werden mich nicht abermals täuschen, wie Sie gewöhnlich zu thun pflegen

happy he who expects little, he will not find himself disappointed wohl dem, der nicht viel erwartet, er wird sich nicht betrogen finden

To dispose.

do what you will, his cunning will know how to disappoint your arrangements thun Sie, was Sie wollen, so wird seine List Ihre Einrichtungen zu vereiteln wissen

so many disappointments in one's life are enough to make one cautious so viele getäuschte Erwartungen (or Täuschungen) im Leben sind geeignet, einen vorsichtig zu machen

To dispose.

I send you enclosed a bill of exchange for £250 at eight days sight of the amount of which you may dispose at your pleasure ich sende Ihnen hiermit einen Wechsel für zwei hundert und funfzig Pfund auf acht Tage Sicht, über dessen Betrag Sie nach Belieben disponiren (or verfügen) können

if I were disposed to suspicion, the manner in which he disposed his guests at table would lead me to believe that there was something particular in the wind wenn ich zu Verdacht geneigt wäre, so würde die Art, wie er seine Gäste am Tische vertheilte, mich zu dem Glauben verleiten, daß etwas Ungewöhnliches im Werke ist

every thing in the British Museum is disposed in the best possible order alles im Brittischen Museum ist in der bestmöglichen Ordnung eingerichtet und aufgestellt

an absolute owner of a property may dispose of it in his will to whomever he pleases ein unbeschränkter Eigenthümer einer Besitzung kann dieselbe vermachen wem er will

if the favourite could dispose the monarch to recall this obnoxious ordonance, the nation would be inclined to forgive him much of his former malpractices wenn der Günstling den Monarchen dahin bringen (or vermögen, or bereden) könnte, daß er diese verhaßte Verordnung zurücknähme, so würde die Nation geneigt seyn, ihm vieles von seinen früheren schlechten Streichen zu verzeihen

I should like you to dispose of your time more usefully than you generally do ich wünschte sehr, daß Sie Ihre Zeit nützlicher anwendeten, als Sie gewöhnlich zu thun pflegen if I were at all disposed to laugh to-day, the manner in which you disposed of your carriage and horses would make me laugh outright wenn ich heute ja zum Lachen aufgelegt wäre, so würde die Art, wie Sie Ihren Wagen und Pferde verkauft (or losgeschlagen) haben, mich laut lachen machen

I have just called on Miss F.— to take her out with me for a drive, but I found she was not disposed to leave her room ich bin so eben bei Fräulein F.— vorgefahren, um Sie auf eine Spazierfahrt mitzunehmen, aber ich fand, daß Sie keine Lust hatte, ihr Zimmer zu verlassen

To do.

you do little or nothing from morning till night Sie thun wenig oder nichts vom Morgen bis in die Nacht

what have you to do with that? was haben Sie damit zu thun (or schaffen) — or was geht das Sie an?

what one does willingly, one does easily was man gern thut, thut man leicht

do right, and fear no one thue Recht und scheue niemand(en)

do what you are bidden; and never do such a thing again thue, was man dir befiehlt; und thue dergleichen nie wieder

here is nothing farther to be done *hier läßt sich nichts weiter thun (or machen)*

when you have done all, you are but an unprofitable servant wenn du alles gethan hast, so bist du doch nur ein fauler Knecht

you should do here, as if you were at home Sie sollten hier thun, als wenn Sie zu Hause wären

all my work is done alle meine Arbeit ist gethan (or vollendet)

how is this coat to be done? wie wollen Sie diesen Rock gemacht haben?

do it, as it is now the fashion machen Sie ihn, wie es jetzt Mode ist

if you do these clothes well, you shall in future always work for me wenn Sie diese Kleider gut machen, so sollen Sie künftig immer für mich arbeiten the matter is now done, and I have nothing farther to do with it die Sache ist nun zu Ende (or vorüber), und ich habe nichts weiter damit zu thun (or schaffen)

now that the mischief is done, all that you can say will not do nun da das Unglück geschehen ist, hilft alles, was Sie sagen können, zu nichts

well, that may do nun, das mag angehen

that won't do das geht (or paßt) nicht or das kann nicht seyn

it may do elsewhere anderswo mag es angehen

you have done very well by him Sie haben sehr gut an ihm gehandelt

I can lend you a few pounds, if they will do ich kann Ihnen einige Pfund leihen, wenn das genug ist (or hinreicht)

as soon as he had done speaking, he left the hall sobald er mit seiner Rede zu Ende war, verließ er den Saal

will you soon have done? sind Sie bald fertig?

one letter is done ein Brief ist fertig (or geschrieben)

this picture must have been done by an experienced artist dieses Gemälde muß von einem erfahrenen Künstler gemahlt seyn (or herrühren)

I don't know what to do with this incorrigible youth ich weiß nicht, was ich mit diesem ausgelassenen Jüngling anfangen soll

pray, have done with your teazing hören Sie doch einmal auf einen zu quälen

let me know, when the service is done lassen Sie mich's wissen, wenn die Kirche aus (or der Gottesdienst vorüber) ist

a little present to the secretary will do your business ein kleines Geschenk an den Secretär gemacht, und Sie haben gewonnen Spiel

they do not do much business in that street in jener Straße giebt es nicht viel Kundschaft

they have done us much good sie haben uns viel Gutes erwiesen

is the meat done? ist das Fleisch gar?

I do not like my food under-done ich mag nicht mein Essen halb gar (or halb gekocht)

these easterly winds will do for me diese Ostwinde werden mich umbringen (kill) now that you have let your toy fall, it is done for nun, ba bu dein Spielzeug haſt fallen laſſen, iſt es zerbrochen

will these handkerchiefs do for you? ſind dieſe Taſchentücher nach Ihrem Wunſche?

XCIII. When the object of an action is stated as a secondary result, or if we do not wish to move participles or infinitives too far from the nominative, the object, preceded by zwar (indeed), is brought in after the participle, etc. See an example, in p. 121.

XCIV. *How* after an infin. is not translated. See example p. 125.

XCV. *To do* used to prevent the repetition of a verb is not rendered; the second verb being either repeated, or dropped altogether. Thus:

No one could have received me better than he did niemand hätte mich beſſer aufnehmen (or empfangen) können, als er

you promised me you would not go out, if it rained, and now you have done it ſie verſprachen mir, Sie wollten nicht ausgehen, wenn es regnen ſollte; und nun ſind ſie doch ausgegangen

we ought to care for the interest of others, as we do for our own wir ſollten für den Vortheil anderer eben ſo beſorgt ſeyn, als wir es für unſern eigenen ſind

did he really say so? hat er es wirklich geſagt?

yes, he did ja or ja freilich (or, repeating) ja, er hat es wirklich geſagt

N.B. The same rule applies to the verbs *to have*, and *to be*. Thus:

has your brother got his commission? Yes, he has hat Ihr Bruder ſeine Anſtellung (or Beſtallung) erhalten? Ja, (or ja, er hat ſie erhalten)

no, he has not nein (or nein, er hat ſie (noch) nicht erhalten

has the concert begun? yes, it has hat das Concert angefangen? ja, (or ja, es hat angefangen)

is this not a very pretty dress? Yes, it is iſt dies nicht ein ſehr hübſches Kleid? Ja, or ja wohl (or ja, es iſt recht hübſch)

To draw.

your horses draw this carriage easily Ihre Pferde ziehen diesen Wagen leicht

how do they draw the water from such a deep well? wie zieht man das Wasser aus einem so tiefen Brunnen?

the barbarian drew his sword and raised it over the head of his disarmed enemy der Barbar zog sein Schwert und zückte es über dem Haupte seines entwaffneten Feindes

one corps drew up the hill and the other down into the valley Ein Corps* (or Eine Schaar) zog den Berg hinauf, und das andere hinunter in's Thal

his inordinate vanity drew him into ruin seine grenzenlose Eitelkeit zog ihn in's Verderben

this plaister does not draw dieses Pflaster zieht nicht

a clever diplomatist draws his advantage from every accidental event ein geschickter Diplomatiker zieht aus jeder Zufälligkeit Vortheil

he will know too how to draw himself out (extricate himself) from unforeseen difficulties er weiß auch, wie er sich aus unvorhergesehenen Schwierigkeiten zu ziehen hat

his fate is drawing to a close sein Schicksal zieht sich seinem Ende zu (or entgegen)

in proportion as our troops drew forward, those of the enemy drew back so wie unsere Truppen heranzogen (or rückten), zogen sich die des Feindes (or die feindlichen) zurück

knowing him to be a distinguished scholar, we tried every thing in our power to draw him out, but it was all in vain. He drew his chair close to the fire, drew a book out of his pocket, and there he sat reading to himself, till it was time for every one to go to bed da wir wußten, daß er ein ausgezeichneter Gelehrter ist, so versuchten wir alles mögliche, ihn zum Sprechen zu bringen, aber es war alles vergebens. Er zog seinen Stuhl

---

* Pronounced as in English.

dicht an's Feuer, zog (or nahm) ein Buch aus der Tasche, und saß da und las, bis es Zeit war, daß jeder zu Bette ginge

why should you endure all this pain, if having your decayed tooth drawn, would give you relief at once warum sollten Sie all diesen Schmerz leiden, da, wenn Sie sich Ihren hohlen Zahn ausreißen ließen, Sie auf einmal Ruhe haben würden

tell my man to draw some beer sagen Sie meinem Bedienten, er solle etwas Bier zapfen

whence could the ancient Egyptians have drawn their science, if not from India? woher konnten die alten Egyptier ihre Wissenschaft geholt haben, wenn nicht von (or aus) Indien?

I am afraid these birds have never been drawn ich fürchte, diese Vögel sind gar nicht ausgeweidet worden

the regiment drew up in front of the royal palace das Regiment stellte sich vor dem königlichen Palaste auf

the noise continued till the curtain drew up der Lärm dauerte fort, bis der Vorhang auf (or in die Höhe) ging

Kean used to draw as large houses as Kemble Kean pflegte das Theater eben so sehr anzufüllen (or ein eben so großes Auditorium heranzuziehen) als Kemble

have the agreement immediately drawn up by a notary lassen Sie den Vertrag sogleich von einem Notar(ius) aufsetzen

their zeal for the propagation of the holy scriptures drew upon them a persecution on the part of the priests ihr Eifer für die Verbreitung der heiligen Schrift brachte ihnen eine Verfolgung von Seiten der Pfaffen zuwege (or zog ihnen....zu)

if you pull it hard, you may draw it out considerably wenn Sie es stark anziehen, so können Sie es bedeutend verlängern

the sum which you drew on me the 5th ultimo will be duly honoured die Summe, welche Sie am fünften vorigen Monats auf mich trassirt (or gezogen) haben, wird gebührend honorirt werden

can you draw? zeichnen Sie?

a good painter ought to draw every thing from nature ein guter Mahler sollte alles nach der Natur zeichnen

I will show you all the drawings I have in my port-folio ich will Ihnen alle die Zeichnungen zeigen (or Sie .... sehen lassen), die ich in meiner Mappe habe

how many feet of water does this ship draw, when she has her full cargo? wie viele Schuh (or Fuß) tief geht dieses Schiff im Wasser, wann es seine volle Ladung hat?

this book is drawing to a close dieses Buch nähert sich seinem Ende (or Schlusse)

Participles after Prepositions.*

if you once accustom yourself to getting up early, you will find no difficulty in it wenn Sie sich einmal daran gewöhnen, früh aufzustehen (or an's frühe Aufstehen gewöhnen), so werden Sie keine Schwierigkeit mehr darin finden

although he is proud of being able to drink more than any one else, I am sure, no one will envy him for this accomplishment obgleich er stolz darauf ist, daß er mehr trinken kann als irgend ein anderer, so wird ihn doch gewiß niemand um diesen Vorzug beneiden

I could not help smiling at being taken for a foreigner ich konnte nicht umhin, (darüber) zu lächeln, daß man mich für einen Ausländer hielt

don't you rejoice at being at last released from so pernicious a position? freuen Sie sich nicht darüber (or freut es Sie nicht), daß Sie endlich von einem so schädlichen Verhältniß[57] befreiet sind

she was dreadfully startled on hearing of my intention sie entsetzte sich, als sie vernahm, was meine Absicht war

---

* See Remark XCII, p. 118.

[57] Also *circumstance, relation*; from verhalten *to hold, be related*. Hence it also signifies *proportion*, as we say zwei verhält sich zu vier, wie vier zu acht two bears the same relation (proportion) to 4, as 4 to 8.

I recognised him immediately by his peculiar manner of taking off his hat ich erkannte ihn sogleich an der eigenthümlichen Art, wie er den Hut abnimmt

by respecting the rights of others, you will make yours to be respected indem (or wenn) Sie die Rechte anderer achten, werden Sie machen, daß man die Ihrigen achtet

a good man finds his greatest enjoyment in doing good to others ein guter Mann findet seinen Genuß darin, wenn er anderen Gutes thun kann

I never doubted your being able to repay the loan you wanted, and I fully relied on your doing it at the proper time ich zweifelte nie daran, daß Sie würden die Anleihe zurückbezahlen können, und verließ mich gänzlich darauf, daß sie es zur gehörigen Zeit thun würden

Peculiar Uses of Prepositions.

I am astonished *at* nothing ich wundre mich (or erstaune) über nichts

you may sneer *at* my credulity, but I have more reason to be angry *at* your unbelief Sie mögen über meine Leichtgläubigkeit spötteln, aber ich habe mehr Ursache über Ihren Unglauben zu zürnen

I can only rejoice to hear you now making game *of* that *at* which you formerly used to tremble ich kann mich nur darüber freuen, daß ich Sie sich jetzt über das lustig machen sehe, wovor Sie ehemals zu zittern pflegten

why should you be frightened *at* that which is so truly harmless? warum sollten sie vor dem zittern, was so wahrhaft harmlos ist

one may now send books as well as letters *by* post man kann jetzt sowohl Bücher als Briefe durch die Post schicken

Harold was in the battle *of* Hastings first wounded *by* an arrow which struck his eye Harald wurde in der Schlacht bei Hastings zuerst durch einen Pfeil verwundet, der ihn im Auge traf the nation was released from a tyrant by a murder die Nation wurde durch einen Mord von einem Tyrannen befreit

there are people who are scandalised at (or by) trifles es giebt Leute, die sich an Kleinigkeiten stoßen (or an Kleinigkeiten Anstoß nehmen)

I have known this long ago *by* (or *from*) dire experience ich weiß dies schon längst aus trauriger Erfahrung

we ought not to condemn our neighbour on mere suspicion wir sollten unsern Nächsten[58] nicht auf bloßen Verdacht hin verdammen

I acted entirely *by* your advice and direction ich handelte gänzlich nach Ihrem Rath und nach Ihrer Vorschrift

for particular reasons and *from* respect for my superiors, I could not make the communication to you at the time you seemed so anxiously to expect it aus besondern Gründen und aus Achtung vor meinen Vorgesetzten, konnte ich Ihnen die Mittheilung nicht zur Zeit machen, wo Sie solche (or dieselbe) so begierig zu erwarten schienen

if you do not know these things *from* experience, you will never learn them *from* books wenn Sie solche Dinge nicht aus Erfahrung wissen, so werden Sie sie nie aus Büchern lernen

a boy who will run away *from* a little dog is too timid *for* a soldier; and one who can not climb a tree is not fit *for* a sailor ein Knabe, der v o r einem kleinen Hündchen davon läuft, ist zu schüchtern zum Soldaten; und einer, der nicht auf einen Baum zu klettern versteht, taugt nicht zum Matrosen (or Seemann)

I was to travel *for* pleasure after I had long ceased to find pleasure *in* travelling ich sollte zum Vergnügen reisen, nachdem ich längst aufgehört hatte am Reisen Vergnügen zu finden

if you dawdle about much longer, you will be too late *for* the meeting wenn Sie noch viel

---

[58] Neighbour in the sense of *one living near* Nachbar; but in the scriptural sense it is Nächster, the superlative degree of the adj. nah, *near;* and is declined like every other adjective.

länger herum kriechen, so kommen Sie zu spät für die (or zur) Versammlung

he who is anxious *for* his advancement in the world must always be ready *for* action wenn es um sein Fortkommen in der Welt zu thun ist, muß zu jeder Zeit zum Handeln bereit seyn

although we are all inclined *for* peace, prudence demands that we should make the most efficient preparations *for* defence obgleich wir alle zum Frieden geneigt sind, so erfordert (doch) die Klugheit, daß wir die tüchtigsten Anstalten zur Vertheidigung treffen

the corn[59] being ready *for* cutting, it behoves us to make speedy preparations *for* the harvest da das Getreide zum Schneiden reif ist, so geziemt es uns schleunige Anstalten zur Ernte (or Aernbte) zu treffen

she had hoped *for* a better reception, and was not prepared *for* such rudeness from a person *for* whose company she had so long desired sie hatte auf einen bessern Empfang gehofft, und war nicht auf eine solche Grobheit (or Rohheit) von einer Person vorbereitet, nach deren Gesellschaft (or Umgang) sie sich so lange gesehnt hatte

they were anxious *for* an opportunity to court the influential man's favour sie waren begierig nach einer Gelegenheit um des einflußreichen Mannes Gunst buhlen zu können

he has now to mourn *for* the loss of her whom he had courted *for* many years er hat jetzt um den Verlust derjenigen zu trauern, um die er viele Jahre lang geworben (or er sich .... beworben) hatte

I will play, if it is a pleasure to you; but I must tell you that I never play for money ich will spielen, wenn Ihnen damit ein Gefallen geschieht; aber ich muß Ihnen sagen, daß ich nie um Geld spiele

---

[59] Getreide means any kind of cereals; Korn any grain or seed. In some parts of Germany it is applied to rye; as cabbage is emphatically called Kraut (herb). *It is* however not applied, as in this country, to oats, which is Hafer (always used in the sing.)

a musician who gets paid for his playing on an instrument, plays for money ein Musiker (or Tonkünstler), der sich für sein Spielen auf irgend einem Instrumente bezahlen läßt, spielt für Geld

many prefer to beg *for* their maintenance rather than to work *for* it viele ziehen es vor, um ihren Unterhalt zu betteln, als dafür zu arbeiten

to hide a danger *from* a man is not removing it eine Gefahr vor einem Menschen zu verbergen heißt nicht sie beseitigen

the best wines are made *from* the pure juice of the grape, without any additions whatever die besten Weine werden aus dem reinen Saft der Traube gemacht, und zwar ohne irgend eine andere Zuthat

how can a country be said to decrease *in* wealth and prosperity, so long as it adds to the comforts and well-being of life? wie läßt sich sagen, daß ein Land an Reichthum und Wohlstand abnimmt, so lange sich dessen Bequemlichkeiten und Wohlbehagen vermehren?

a people may be poor *in* money, yet rich *in* every enjoyment ein Volk mag arm an Geld und doch reich an allen Genüssen seyn

this prince[60] must be very great *in* power, if he is to be superior *in* forces to such wealthy and vigorous neighbours dieser Fürst muß sehr groß an Macht seyn, wenn er solchen reichen und energischen Nachbarn an Kräften überlegen seyn soll

every Englishman abroad has a right to expect protection *in* the diplomatic agents of his country, whether they be called consuls, chargé d'affaires, or ambassadors jeder Engländer im Auslande hat ein Recht Schutz an den diplomatischen Agenten seines Vaterlandes zu finden, gleichviel ob dieselben (or solche) Consulen, Geschäftsträger oder Gesandte genannt werden

there is no disputing on such a point with one who does not believe *in* virtue es läßt sich mit

---

[60] A reigning prince, or one who bears a title as such is called Fürst; the son of a sovereign, Prinz. Princess, respectively, Fürstinn and Prinzessinn.

einem Menschen über einen solchen Punkt nicht streiten, der nicht an Tugend glaubt

trust *in* the justice of your cause, and persevere *in* your first resolution vertrauen Sie auf die Gerechtigkeit Ihrer Sache, und beharren Sie bei Ihrem ersten Entschluß

he who is engaged *in* a useful employment should keep to it, unless he were able to do something really better wer sich mit einer nützlichen Sache beschäftigt, sollte dabei bleiben, er müßte benn* etwas wahrhaft besseres thun können

if the money is of real service to you, it will afford me great pleasure to lend it to you wenn Ihnen mit dem Gelde wirklich gedient ist, so werde ich mir ein großes Vergnügen daraus machen, es Ihnen zu leihen

on such occasions we like to go *into* the country bei solchen Gelegenheiten gehen wir gern auf's Land

we were conversing the whole evening *on* the expediency of sending the young man *to* College wir sprachen (or unterhielten uns) den ganzen Abend über die Räthlichkeit den jungen Menschen auf die Universität zu senden (or schicken)

my mother lived *in* the country all the time I was *at* College meine Mutter lebte auf dem Lande die ganze Zeit über, wo ich auf der hohen Schule war

we will go out *into* the field, to see the new plough tried wir wollen auf's Feld hinaus gehen, um den neuen Pflug probiren zu sehen

the whole time that the miscreant was *on* board the ship, he thought *of* nothing but how he might be revenged *on* the poor youth by whom he thought himself offended die ganze Zeit über, wo der Elende sich auf dem Schiffe befand, dachte er an nichts als, wie er sich an dem armen Jüngling rächen möchte, von dem er sich beleidigt wähnte

the tale borders very closely *on* the impossible die Erzählung grenzt sehr nahe an's Unmögliche

it was prohibited *on* pain of death to appear armed *in* the streets

---

* Notice this idiom for *unless*.

es war bei Todesstrafe verboten, bewaffnet auf den Straßen zu erscheinen

although they might have made the journey *by* water or *on* horseback, they rather made it *on* foot obgleich sie hätten die Reise zu Wasser oder zu Pferde machen können, machten Sie sie lieber zu Fuße

he might indeed have died *of* his fever, yet he actually died with (or of) cold and hunger er hätte freilich an seinem Fieber sterben können, aber er starb wirklich vor Kälte und Hunger

it is as possible to die *with* joy as *with* grief es ist eben so möglich vor Freude, als vor Kummer zu sterben

pray, stay to-night *with* us; why, it is quite impossible to walk *with* such a wind bleiben Sie doch heute Nacht bei uns; es ist ja ganz unmöglich bei einem solchen Winde zu Fuße zu gehen

on the contrary, I shall walk all the faster im Gegentheil, ich werde nur um so schneller gehen

do not press him any farther. Our good friend likes to be excentric, and says these kind of things *on* purpose. The more you urge him to stay, the more he will insist on going bringen Sie nicht weiter in ihn. Unser guter Freund spielt gern den Sonderling und sagt dergleichen Dinge mit Fleiß. Je mehr Sie in ihn bringen (or ihn nöthigen) zu bleiben, desto mehr wird er darauf bestehen, wegzugehen

if you will sell to this person *on* credit, I shall not interfere *with* it wenn Sie diesem Menschen auf Credit (or Borg) verkaufen wollen, so werde ich mich nicht drein mischen

although he passes himself for my nephew, I do not consider it right to acknowledge a person as such of whom I know absolutely nothing except what he chuses to state of himself obgleich er sich für meinen Neffen ausgiebt, so halte ich es doch nicht für Recht, einen Menschen als solchen anzuerkennen, von dem ich durchaus nichts weiß, als was er von sich selbst auszusagen für gut findet (or beliebt)

as soon as the court had declared him innocent, he again passed with every body for an honest

man fobald das Gericht ihn für unschuldig erklärt hatte, galt er wieder bei jedermann für einen ehrlichen Mann
I always thought him a man of honour, and am delighted that you also have found him to be such ich habe ihn immer für einen Ehrenmann gehalten, und es freuet mich ungemein, daß Sie ihn auch als solchen erkannt haben

XCVI. Dieselbe or dieselben or solche may be used after Sie to avoid the repetition of the same word.

XCVII. Dessen or deren, desselben or derselben are often used instead of the possessive pronoun, when the object is to show that the possessor is the *last* person spoken of, or an animal or inanimate object.

XCVIII. He who derjenige (or der) welcher ⎫
she who diejenige (or die) welche ⎬ or wer
they who diejenigen (or die) welche ⎭
that which dasjenige (or das) welches, or was.

Derjenige, etc., is declined like every other adjective preceded by the def. art, and wer makes the Gen. wessen, the Dat. wem and the Acc. wen.

A personal or demonstr. pron. preceding a relative pron. or the latter preceding a subst. followed by such a pronoun is rendered by derjenige etc., or bei der, die, das, with the Gen. dessen and deren and the Plur. denen. When he who, she who, etc. mean *whoever, whatever*, and thus do not refer to any particular individual or individuals, wer is preferred.

XCIX. Wo like *où* in French, is often used for daß, in welchem, auf welchem etc.

C. *In, at, into* and *to* relating to Straße street, Universität, Akademie, hohe Schule university, Stadthaus townhouse, Tanzsaal dancing room, Schiff ship, Land country (in opposition to town), Feld field, Wiese meadow, are rendered by auf, governing the Dat. when indicating a place of stay, and the Acc. when they express the point at which a motion or tendency terminates. Yet when Land means *land or realm* and Feld is used with reference to war those prepos. *are rendered by* in.

Accessory Clauses turned into Adjectives.

the stranger whom you accompanied turns out to be an old acquaintance of ours der Fremde, welchen Sie begleiteten (or der von Ihnen begleitete Fremde) erweist sich als ein alter Bekannter von uns

the prints which you ordered for me at Colnaghi's, are not yet arrived die Kupferstiche, die Sie für mich bei Calnaghi bestellt haben (or die von Ihnen für mich bei Calnaghi bestellten Kupferstiche) sind noch nicht angekommen

the house which your upholsterer had so nicely furnished and fitted up for us, has been unfortunately burnt down das Haus, welches Ihr Möblirer so hübsch für uns möblirt und eingerichtet hatte (or das von Ihrem ...... möblirte und eingerichtete Haus), ist unglücklicher Weise abgebrannt)

the brisk commerce which has lately sprung up between this country and Belgium is likely to prove profitable to both countries der thätige Verkehr, welcher seit kurzem zwischen diesem Lande und Belgien entstanden ist (or der seit ... entstandene thätige Verkehr) wird sich für beide Länder vortheilhaft erweisen

these two children who are so much like each other are not in the least related diese beiden Kinder, welche einander so ähnlich sehen (or diese beiden ... sehenden Kinder) sind nicht im entferntesten mit einander verwandt

the somewhat narrow and by no means splendid streets are beautifully paved, and the large squares, planted with high and noble trees, are surrounded with magnificent houses die etwas engen und keinesweges prächtigen Straßen sind vortrefflich gepflastert, und die großen mit hohen und herrlichen Bäumen besetzten Plätze [61] sind mit prachtvollen Häusern umgeben

this great general, so celebrated in the last war, and so much esteemed for his justice and

---

[61] Platz, like the French *place*, means any open space in a town surrounded with houses.

humanity, yielded at last to the weakness which besets human nature under every form dieser große, im letzten Kriege so berühmte, und durch seine Gerechtigkeit und Menschlichkeit so ausgezeichnete General (or Feldherr) gab zuletzt der, der menschlichen Natur in allen ihren Gestalten anklebenden Schwäche nach

CI. This form of composition arises from clauses dependent on substantives (the relative pronoun and auxiliary verb having been first thrown off) being placed before those substantives with which the last word, which is always a participle or adjective, is made to agree. They are, as will have been seen, not indispensable. Yet they frequently occur both in writing and speaking, and should therefore be studied.

Conjunctions.

- how great soever his party may be, he is subject to the law like the meanest peasant in the land so (or wie) groß auch sein Anhang seyn mag, so ist er doch, wie der gemeinste Bauer im Lande, dem Gesetz unterworfen

- however gentle a cat may seem, it is an animal which is not to be trusted so (or wie) fromm auch eine Katze scheinen mag, sie (or es) ist ein Thier, dem nicht zu trauen ist

- whoever it may be, and from whence soever he may come, if any one calls here this afternoon, I do not wish to see him wer es auch sey, und woher er auch komme, wenn jemand heute Nachmittag hier zuspricht, so will ich ihn nicht sehen

- wherever Englishmen are settled, they are sure to establish before all things a newspaper wo nur immer Engländer sich niederlassen, so ist gewiß eine Zeitung das allererste, was sie zu gründen pflegen

- in case you should doubt my word, I can assure you that what I told you is believed by even the most educated people in the neighbourhood falls Sie mein Wort bezweifeln sollten, so kann ich Sie versichern, daß was ich Ihnen gesagt habe, von den gebildetsten Leuten in der Gegend geglaubt wird

as you wear no boots and the country about here is very swampy, I would advise you to wear over-shoes and gaiters da Sie keine Stiefeln tragen, und die Umgegend sehr sumpfig ist, so würde ich Ihnen rathen, Oberschuhe und Gamaschen zu tragen

when would you wish me to put them on? wann wollen Sie, daß ich sie anziehen soll?

I will let you know, when you ought to put them on ich will Sie es wissen lassen, wann Sie sie anziehen sollten

when I got into the arbour, I sat down and took off my wet shoes and stockings als ich in die Laube kam, setzte ich mich nieder und zog meine nassen Schuhe und Strümpfe aus

when one is hot and in perspiration one ought not to sit down in a draught wenn einem heiß ist und man schwitzt, sollte man sich nicht in einen Zug setzen

when I meet the judge, I take off my hat silently and pass on wenn (or wann) ich dem Richter begegne, so nehme ich schweigend den Hut ab, und gehe weiter

when I met the colonel, I took off my hat als ich dem Obristen begegnete, nahm ich den Hut ab

having transferred your claims to the inheritance to another, you ought no further to meddle in the matter nachdem Sie Ihre Ansprüche auf die Erbschaft auf einen andern übertragen haben, sollten Sie sich nicht weiter in die Sache mischen

you should have thought of all this, before you took so important a step Sie hätten an alles dieses denken sollen, ehe Sie einen so wichtigen Schritt thaten

the more noise you now make, the more people will blame you for your precipitancy, and will ask you, whether you ought not to have reflected upon the risk you ran, when you were about signing so important a document je mehr Lärm Sie jetzt machen, je (or desto) mehr wird man Ihre Hast tadeln, und Sie fragen, ob Sie nicht hätten die Gefahr, welche Sie liefen, bedenken sollen, als Sie im Begriffe standen, ein so wichtiges Document zu unterschreiben

I have had this habit from my childhood, and have retained

it, because no one ever made me aware of it, how habits, seemingly innocent, may prove pernicious to oneself as well as to others ich habe diese Gewohnheit seit meiner Kindheit (or von Kindheit auf), und habe sie beibehalten, weil niemand mich je darauf aufmerksam gemacht hat, wie dem Anscheine nach unschuldige Gewohnheiten uns selbst sowohl als andern nachtheilig (or schädlich) werden können

no sooner was the messenger arrived, than the whole family were assembled nicht sobald war der Bot(h)e angekommen, als die ganze Familie zusammenberufen ward

as long as you remain in town, you must stay in my house, altho' I may myself be occasionally obliged to be absent for a few days so lange (als) Sie in der Stadt bleiben, müssen Sie bei mir wohnen, wenn ich auch selbst gelegentlich genöthigt seyn sollte, mich auf ein paar Tagen zu entfernen

if the resolution so rashly taken by them is to be carried out, I will not answer for the consequences wenn der von ihnen so rasch gefaßte Beschluß ausgeführt werden soll (or soll der ..... ausgeführt werden), so will (or mag) ich nicht für die Folgen einstehen

go with us as far as the toll-gate, if you are not too tired gehen Sie mit bis an das Zollgatter, so Sie nicht zu müde sind

CII. If by *when* we wish to ascertain a time, it must be rendered by wann; if to fix a time by a circumstance already known, by als; if an habitual time, by wenn.

CIII. Da *as, when, since* (being a conjunction) moves the verb to the end. Da signifying *then, here,* or *there* (being an adverb), when placed at the beginning of a clause, moves the nominative after the verb. The same is respectively the case with so, the conjunction, signifying *however, soever, if;* or so, the adverb, meaning *thus.*

CIV. The conjunction *before* is bevor or ehe, the preposition vor; *the conjunction since,* usually seitdem, the preposition seit; the conjunction *after,* nachdem, the preposition nach.

CONJUNCTIONS. 143

CV. Als after sobald as soon as, so lang as long as, and so weit as far as, is usually omitted.

CVI. Wenn and daß (if and that) are often omitted and in the case of the former the Nom. always placed after the verb; and of the latter the verb not moved to the end.

CVII. *Although* is rendered by obschon, obgleich, obwohl, ob auch, wenn gleich, wenn schon, wenn auch, wiewohl, wie auch, of which the first two are the most common. Gleich, wohl, auch are often separated from the first particle. Sometimes too the first, and sometimes the second particle is omitted.

CONJUNCTIONS (CONTINUED).

in what capacity does Mr. N. go to the Brazils? is it as a mere traveller or as a naturalist? als was geht Herr N. nach Brasilien? ist es als bloßer Reisender, oder als Naturforscher?

men will sometimes behave as (or like) heroes, who are cowards at heart manche Menschen benehmen sich zuweilen wie Helden, welche im Herzen Feiglinge sind

he is as learned as his father, and nearly as good looking as his mother er ist so gelehrt als sein Vater, und beinahe so hübsch wie seine Mutter

he was indeed every one's favourite, yet he never presumed upon it er war freilich bei jedermann beliebt, dieses machte ihn jedoch nicht anmaßend

there have been indeed more prosperous times; but I do not know of any, when there was more honesty in the world es hat zwar glücklichere Zeiten gegeben; aber ich wüßte keine, wo es mehr Rechtlichkeit in der Welt gegeben hätte

either you must be able to command, or you must obey man muß entweder befehlen können, oder man muß gehorchen

you either give yourself up to despair, or you are extravagantly merry Sie überlassen sich entweder der Verzweiflung, oder sind ausgelassen lustig he was certainly no genius; but he had common sense er war freilich kein Genie, aber er hatte gefunden Menschenverstand

he also wrote no verses; but devoted his time to his mother's business auch schrieb er keine Gedichte, sondern widmete seine Zeit seiner Mutter Geschäfte.

nor was his father more distinguished as a literary man; for he made during his whole life nothing but shoes and boots auch war sein Vater nicht ausgezeichnet als Gelehrter, denn er machte in seinem ganzen Leben nichts als Schuhe und Stiefeln

but he was nevertheless highly respected in his day allein er stand dennoch zu seiner Zeit in hoher Achtung

he was in fact a senator of his little town; and not only a sagacious justice of the peace, but also a promoter of the general prosperity of his corporation er war nämlich Senator (or Rathsherr) seines Städtchens und nicht nur ein scharfsichtiger Friedensrichter, sondern auch ein Beförderer des allgemeinen Wohlstandes seiner Corporation

otherwise I know nothing about him, except that he lived to a goodly old age sonst weiß ich nichts von ihm, nur (or außer) daß er ein ziemlich hohes Alter erreichte

we judge of people rightly or not according to our knowledge of them and of the world in general wir beurtheilen die Menschen billig oder nicht, je nachdem wir sie kennen und je nach dem Umfange unserer Menschenkenntniß überhaupt

we ought not only to be just, but even generous wir sollten nicht nur (or bloß) gerecht, sondern auch (or sogar) großmüthig seyn

however also in this case much that glitters is not gold, and much that would pass for magnanimity may be but selfishness in disguise indessen ist auch hier manches das glänzt, nicht Gold; und vieles welches für Großmuth gelten möchte, ist vielleicht nichts als vermummte Selbstsucht

nevertheless there are virtuous people, and consequently, he is not to be admired who would represent all goodness as the

effect of a clever calculation nichts desto weniger giebt es tugendhafte Menschen, und derjenige ist keinesweges zu loben, der alle Güte für die Wirkung einer klugen Berechnung ausgeben möchte

CVIII. Als expresses identity, wie similarity or an approximation to it.

CIX. *Indeed* is rendered by freilich, when it means *to be sure*; by zwar, when it signifies *it is true*; by in der That, when it stands for *in fact*.

CX. *But* is usually rendered by aber, or allein; if it expresses a stronger contrast, by doch; but when it introduces a clause which states that a person, thing or action is quite the opposite of that stated before, it is represented by sondern.

CXI. When *nor* begins a clause, it is rendered by auch followed by a negation.

Wohl, ja, doch, denn, schon Used as Expletives.

I suppose you have not experienced such a thing yourself Sie haben wohl dergleichen (or so etwas, or etwas dieser Art) nicht selbst erfahren

I dare say, I could forward such an object, if I would at all meddle with railway-shares ich könnte wohl solch einen Zweck befördern, wenn ich mich überhaupt mit Eisenbahn-Aktien befassen wollte

mind, you don't mentoin this to a speculator nehmen Sie sich ja in Acht, daß Sie dieses gegen keinen Spekulanten erwähnen (or erwähnen Sie dieses ja gegen ......)!

you surely will not confine your benevolence to so small a circle! Sie werden doch Ihre Wohlthätigkeit nicht auf einen so engen Kreis beschränken wollen!

how can you judge so uncharitably? wie können Sie denn (or doch) so lieblos urtheilen?

can he really laugh at this? kann er denn wirklich darüber lachen?

mind you let me hear of you, as soon as you reach the place of your destination	laſſen Sie mich ja von Ihnen hören, ſo bald Sie Ihren Beſtimmungsort erreicht haben
do take more pains in future	geben Sie ſich doch in Zukunft mehr Mühe
so we will let it rest	es bleibt denn (or alſo) dabei
I suppose you have been waiting a good while for me?	Sie warten wohl ſchon lange auf mich?
how you can ask! you know that I was to leave home at 6 o'clock. so you may easily calculate, how long I must have been here	wie Sie fragen können! Sie wiſſen ja, daß ich um ſechs Uhr von Hauſe weggehen ſollte, und können alſo wohl leicht berechnen, wie lange ich ſchon hier ſeyn muß
you don't think, it is my fault that I have stayed away so long?	Sie glauben doch wohl nicht, daß ich aus eigener Schuld ſo lange ausgeblieben bin?
oh certainly not; you have, I dare say, done your best to be punctual	oh keineswegs; Sie haben wohl ohne Zweifel Ihr möglichſtes gethan, pünktlich zu ſeyn
whatever you may think, there is, I dare say, no one who thinks more of punctuality than I do	was Sie auch glauben mögen, ſo giebt es wohl niemanden, der mehr auf Pünktlichkeit hielte, als ich
why don't you accede to your guardian's wish?	warum willigen Sie denn nicht in Ihres Vormundes Wunſch?
you surely do not imagine that so honorable a man has a sinister motive in advising you?	Sie bilden ſich doch wohl nicht ein, daß ein ſo ehrenvoller Mann einen unredlichen Beweggrund hat, wenn er Ihnen räth?
I shall surely let you know	ich werde es Ihnen ſchon zu wiſſen thun

CXII. Wohl expresses probability; doch either doubt, or entreaty; ja a warning or reproach, indicating, in the latter sense, that a person ought to have known what he has been asking about, or doing what he does not. Denn conveys nearly the same meaning as ja, but is joined most frequently to interrogations. Schon is joined to *the Present*, when used instead of the English Perfect tense; but *also signifies* something like *no doubt*.

List of the Principal Adverbs.

1. Of time, on the question *when*?

yesterday geſtern
yesterday morning, evening, night geſtern Morgen, geſtern Abend, geſtern Nacht
the day before yesterday vorgeſtern or ehegeſtern
to-day heute or heut
this morning, noon, &c. heute Morgen, heute Mittag, u. ſ. w.
to-morrow morgen
to-morrow morning morgen früh
to-morrow evening, &c. morgen Abend, u. ſ. w.
the day after to-morrow übermorgen
in the morning Morgens or des Morgens
one morning, or once on a morning eines Morgens
a week, month, year *ago* vor acht Tagen, vor einem Monate, vor einem Jahre
this day, yesterday, to-morrow, a week, or a fortnight (gone) heute, geſtern, morgen, acht, or vierzehn Tage
to-day a week, a fortnight, a month, twelve months (to come) heute, geſtern, morgen über acht Tage, vierzehn Tage, vier Wochen, or über's Jahr
now-a-days heutigen Tages, heut zu Tage
anciently vor Zeiten, vor Alters
formerly, whilome weiland
down from ancient times von Alters her
formerly ſonſt, ehemals
then, at that time da, damals
at present jetzt
now nun, nunmehr
till now, hitherto bis jetzt, bisher, bis hieher
once, one day einſt, einmal
long ago längſt
lately neulich, vor kurzem, letzthin unlängſt
shortly kürzlich, nächſtens, mit nächſtem, eheſtens
but, just then or just now erſt, eben, ſo eben
but now, but to-day, yesterday, lately erſt eben, erſt heute, geſtern, vor kurzem
from this day *forward* von heute an
already ſchon, bereits
previously vorher, zuvor
subsequently nachher
early früh
at the earliest früheſtens
late ſpät

at the latest spätestens
in good time zeitlich, bei Zeiten
daily täglich, alle Tage
hourly stündlich, alle Stunden
weekly wöchentlich, alle Wochen
monthly monatlich, alle Monate
annually jährlich, alle Jahre
incessantly unaufhörlich
for life lebenslang or lebenslänglich
sometimes bisweilen, zuweilen, manchmal
always immer, allzeit
perpetually ewig, immer und ewig
ever je, jemals

never, nie, niemals
never (prospectively) nimmer
frequently oft, öfters
seldom, rarely selten
in the nick of time eben recht
at the wrong time, *mal apropos* zur Unzeit
every time allemal
not once keinmal
now and then dann und wann
not yet noch nicht
yet, as yet noch
soon bald
as soon as possible baldigst

2. Of place, on the question *where?**

in this country hier zu Lande
at the head oben an
below unten, also used after hier, da, dort, and before an
within drinnen
without draußen
somewhere wo, irgends, irgendwo
nowhere nirgends, nirgendwo
elsewhere sonstwo, anderswo, anderwärts
about here or there hier or da herum

everywhere allerwegen, überall
on the road unterwegs
on the outside, abroad auswärts
inside inwendig
outside (by heart) auswendig
at home zu Hause, daheim
beside hier neben or da neben
between hier or da zwischen
level with the ground, on the ground floor ebener or gleicher Erde

3. Of motion, on the question *wherefrom?* formed with her hither.†

out from there da heraus
from somewhere irgend woher
from nowhere nirgend woher

from somewhere else anderswoher
from all places allenthalben her

---

* See also p. 20 and 21.   † See also p. 22 and 23.

LIST OF THE PRINCIPAL ADVERBS.

4. Of motion, on the question *whereto?* formed with hin thither, and often with ba there, placed before them.

there, thither bahin, borthin	to all places or directions allenthalben hin
(to) no where nirgend hin	
to somewhere else anderswohin	to the right rechts hin
	to the left links hin

5. Of locality or motion, on the question *whereabouts?* or *whereto?* without reference to the person.

on, or to the right rechts	towards the top nach oben zu
on, or to the left links	towards the bottom nach unten zu
across quer, quer über	towards the front or back nach vorne, or hinten zu
forward vorwärts	
backwards, towards the rear rück- or hinterwärts, nach hinten zu	(passing) over oben or darüber weg
upwards aufwärts	(passing) underneath unten or darunter weg
downwards niederwärts	
sideways seitwärts	straight forward gerad' aus, or grade zu
homewards heimwärts	

6. Of place, to denote the spot where the action or motion begins, formed with von, and often followed by an or aus.

from here von hier	from there, &c. von da

7. Of place, to denote the spot where the action or motion ceases; formed by bis until, as far as.

as far as here bis hieher (so weit)	as far as there, &c. bis dahin

8. Of Extent, Number, and Order, on the questions *how much? how often? in*, or *to what degree*.

partly theils	alone allein
mostly, for the most part mehrentheils, größtentheils, meistentheils, meistens	altogether, collectively sämmtlich
	upon the whole, generally überhaupt
singly einzeln	simple, manifold einfach, vielfach

once einmal
firstly erstens, erstlich
first zuerst, anfangs
at last, finally zuletzt, endlich
again wieder
thereupon darauf
at the same time zugleich
particularly, in private besonders
in some measure einigermaßen
farther ferner, weiter
then dann, alsdann
subsequently hernach, nachher
regularly ordentlich
in rows reihenweise
verbally, or from word to word wörtlich, von Wort zu Wort
literally buchstäblich
by degrees nach und nach
gradually allmälig

imperceptibly unvermerkt
for the rest übrigens
besides sonst
in conclusion schließlich
in short, in few words kurz, kürzlich
concisely kurz gefaßt
in detail weitläuftig
diffusely weitschweifig
circumstantially ausführlich, umständlich
mixed durcheinander
helter skelter in confusion drunter und drüber
the wrong side upwards das Unterste zu oberst
wrongly, the hindside foremost (the cart before the horse) verkehrt, das Hinterste zuvörderst

9. Of Occurrence.

perhaps vielleicht
perchance, in any way etwa, irgend
by chance ungefähr, von ungefähr
unexpectedly unversehens, unvermuthet
in one way or another so oder so

happily zum Glück, glücklicherweise
unhappily zum Unglück, unglücklicherweise
at random auf's Gerathewohl
in vain vergebens, vergeblich
for nothing, to no purpose umsonst

10. Of Comparison.

like, as wie, als
as if, as though als ob, als wie, als wenn
just as if eben or gerade ob, or nicht anders als ob, or nicht anders *als wenn*

likewise gleichfalls, ebenfalls
likewise, the like desgleichen
otherwise anders
just so eben so
as—as wie or gleich wie—so

not only—but also nicht nur or nicht allein—sondern auch
at least wenigstens
at farthest längstens
more willingly, rather lieber
by far weit, bei weitem
exactly gerade, eben
equally gleich
likewise gleichfalls
unequally ungleich
the—the je—je, je—desto
proportionably ebenmäßig, gleichmäßig
so much the um so
at most höchstens

11. Of Magnitude and Excess.

very sehr, gar
especially vorzüglich
even sogar
nearly beinahe
too zu, gar zu, allzu
almost fast
extremely, excessively äußerst, höchst, überaus
scarcely kaum
only nur
entirely ganz, gänzlich
visibly zusehends
infinitely unendlich
perceptibly merklich
uncommonly ungemein

12. Of Affirmation and Negation.

yes, indeed, truly ja
just so nicht anders
yes indeed, oh yes ja doch, o ja, ach ja
no nein—not nicht
not even nicht einmal
certainly gewiß, ja gewiß
no such thing (don't say so) nicht doch
indeed, in reality wirklich, fürwahr
by no means mit nichten
truly wahrlich, wahrhaftig
no doubt freilich
not at all gar nicht, ganz und gar nicht
seriously ernstlich
infallibly unfehlbar
absolutely not durchaus nicht or schlechterdings nicht
without doubt ohne Zweifel
certainly, no doubt allerdings
by no means keineswegs
as said before wie gesagt
though, indeed doch

13. Of Interrogation.

where wo
whence woher, von wannen

whereabouts wo herum	you have seen the king zum wievielstenmale sehen Sie den König heute
whither wohin	
which way wohinaus	
which way down wohinunter	when wann
how wie	since when seit wann
how much wie viel	is it not so, or not true (familiarly gelt,) nicht wahr
at what number of repetitions zum wievielstenmal (French, *la quantième de fois*)	
	how now wie nun
	why warum
how many times is it to-day that	wherefore weßwegen

CXIII. Fach or fältig joined to numbers and other numeral terms, corresponds with the English *fold*; as, double zweifach or zweifältig, triple dreifach or dreifältig, fourfold vierfach or vierfältig. Einfältig however means simple in the sense of *silly*.

CXIV. We may say erstens or erstlich; but all other numbers only take ens, as zweitens secondly, drittens thirdly.

Verbs expressed by more than one Word.

to chance zufällig geschehen, kommen, gehen	of England at — wenn Sie im Laufe der Woche zufällig in die Regenten-Straße gehen sollten, so thun Sie mir den Gefallen und bestellen mir ein Exemplar von der neuen Ausgabe (or Auflage) von Macaulay's Geschichte von England bei —
I chanced to meet him in a public room es geschah zufällig, daß ich ihn in einem öffentlichen Saale traf (or ich traf ihn zufällig in u. s. w.)	
if you should chance to go to Regent-Street some day this week, I would thank you to order me a copy of the new *edition of* Macaulay's History	to attend, pay attention, to mind Acht geben
	had you attended to the instruction you received at school,

you would know a great deal more than you do hätten Sie auf das Acht gegeben, was man Ihnen in der Schule lehrte, so würden Sie viel mehr können (or wissen), wie jetzt

to beware sich in Acht nehmen

beware of those who profess themselves to be your friends on the first acquaintance nehmen Sie sich vor denen in Acht, die sich bei der ersten Bekanntschaft für Ihre Freunde ausgeben

to out-law in die Acht erklären

to be declared an out-law was formerly a much more serious business than it is now in die Acht erklärt zu werden war ehemals eine weit bedenklichere Sache als es jetzt ist

formerly an out-law was "forbidden to the friend, allowed to the enemy." Now, he only takes a quiet lodging at Boulogne vormals war ein Geächteter „dem Freund verboten, dem Feind erlaubt." Jetzt miethet er sich bloß ein ruhiges Quartier zu Boulogne

to provision mit Lebensmitteln versehen

to defy trotz bieten

the fortress being now abundantly provisioned, it may defy a long siege da die Festung nun überflüssig mit Lebensmitteln versehen ist, so kann sie einer langen Belagerung trotz bieten

to barb an arrow einen Pfeil mit Widerhaken versehen

the Tartars use long, barbed arrows in their warfare die Tartaren bedienen sich langer mit Widerhaken versehenen Pfeilen in ihren Kriegen

to board die Kost haben or geben

he boards and lodges him for two guineas a week er giebt ihm Kost und Wohnung für zwei Guineen die Woche

don't you also board, where you lodge? haben Sie nicht auch die Kost, wo Sie wohnen?

to hesitate Anstand nehmen, Bedenken tragen

to arrange in Ordnung bringen

to disarrange, to confuse in Unordnung, in Verwirrung bringen

would you hesitate a moment to interfere, if you could rearrange your colleague's affairs? würden Sie einen Augenblick Bedenken tragen, sich einzumischen, wenn Sie Ihres Collegen Angelegenheiten wieder in Ordnung bringen könnten?

to consult zu Rathe ziehen, um Rath fragen

would to God, he had consulted me when something could yet be done for him wollte Gott, er hätte mich um Rath gefragt, als ihm noch zu helfen war

to owe schuldig seyn

do you not owe it to society to publish such an iniquity? sind Sie es nicht der Welt schuldig, daß Sie einen solchen Schurkenstreich bekannt machen?

to give up, make a present zum Besten geben

to make game zum Besten haben

to doubt in Zweifel ziehen

when the young gentleman came of age, there were great rejoicings, and his father gave up to the people in the village a whole hogshead of wine als der junge Herr großjährig wurde, gab es große Freudenbezeugungen, und sein Vater gab dem Dorf ein ganzes Orhoft Wein zum Besten

he pretended that he wanted to consult me on the occasion, but I soon discovered that he only wished to make game of me er gab vor, er wolle mich bei der Gelegenheit zu Rathe ziehen, aber ich entdeckte bald, daß er mich nur zum Besten zu haben wünschte

when he saw that the truth of his statements was doubted, he said no more als er fand, daß die Wahrheit seiner Aussagen in Zweifel gezogen wurde, schwieg (or verstummte) er

to finish fertig machen

to give up Preis geben

to fill voll gießen

to benefit wohlthun

the tailor promises to finish your clothes by this evening der Schneider verspricht, Ihre Kleider heute Abend noch fertig zu machen

the houses of the conspirators were given up to the mob for plunder die Häuser der Verschworenen wurden dem Pöbel zur Plünderung Preis gegeben

the mould not having been completely filled, the vase came out in an imperfect state da die

Form nicht ganz voll gegossen (or gefüllt) war, so kam die Vase unvollständig an's Licht

if one wishes really to benefit the poor, one ought to supply them with what they really need wenn man den Armen wirklich wohlthun will, so sollte man ihnen das geben, was sie wirklich bedürfen

Examples of Prepositions used adverbially.

I rely on him ich baue auf ihn

I endeavour to edify him ich suche ihn aufzubauen

do not bite on this nut beißen Sie nicht auf diese Nuß

do not crack this nut with your teeth beißen Sie diese Nuß nicht mit den Zähnen auf

she tied the bonnet on the bundle sie band den Hut auf das Bündel

why do you not untie the bundle? warum binden Sie das Bündel nicht auf?

the footman brought the boy on his shoulder der Bediente brachte den Knaben auf seiner Schulter

it is wrong of you to aggravate the boy es ist Unrecht von Ihnen, den Knaben aufzubringen

have the goods been taken to the ship? sind die Waaren auf's Schiff gebracht worden?

the privateer brought in two ships der Kaper brachte zwei Schiffe auf

she fell with her head against the ground sie fiel mit dem Kopf auf den Boden

did it not strike you that he gave up his prisoners so soon? fiel es Ihnen nicht auf, daß er seine Gefangenen so früh aufgab?

I wish, you would wait for us ich wollte, Sie warteten auf uns

let the servant wait on us lassen Sie den Bedienten uns aufwarten

I shall wait on you at your office ich werde Ihnen in Ihrem Büreau aufwarten

stand by my side stehen Sie bei mir

assist me stehen Sie mir bei

come after us kommen Sie nach uns

follow us kommen Sie uns nach

I shall obey your injunctions ich werde Ihrer Vorschrift nachkommen read after I have done lesen Sie nach mir

read carefully after me, in order to obtain a correct pronunciation lesen Sie mir sorgfältig nach, damit Sie eine richtige Aussprache bekommen

I will write it down for you, and you must write it after me letter by letter ich will es Ihnen vorschreiben, und Sie müssen es mir einen Buchstaben nach dem andern nachschreiben

my music-master always first plays the pieces he brings me, and then I play them after him mein Musikmeister spielt mir die Stücke, die er mir bringt, immer erst vor, und dann spiele ich sie ihm nach

put the book on the shelf above the large dictionary setzen Sie das Buch auf das Brett über das große Wörterbuch

the horse leapt over the ditch das Pferd setzte über den Graben

how do you translate this passage? wie übersetzen Sie diese Stelle?

the soldiers had to carry the guns over the mountain die Soldaten mußten die Kanonen über den Berg tragen

I have transferred my shares ich habe meine Aktien auf einen andern übertragen

---

MISCELLANEOUS SENTENCES.

the passions of the multitude know no patience die Leidenschaften des Volks (or der Menge) kennen keine Geduld

nothing makes us greater and freer than charity and infinite hope nichts macht uns größer und freier als Menschenliebe und unendliche Hoffnung

we often call that which is very probable and very possible incredible, and rather believe something more incredible wir nennen oft das sehr Wahrscheinliche, das sehr Mögliche unglaublich, um lieber noch etwas Unglaublicheres zu glauben.

it seems often almost necessary to act badly, *in order that* the bad may not think ill of us es wäre oft beinahe nöthig, schlecht zu handeln, damit die Schlechten nicht schlecht von uns denken

while selfish man pursues low ends, he often unconsciously promotes the noblest ends of providence indem der selbstsüchtige Mensch niedrige Zwecke verfolgt, befördert er unbewußt oft die vortrefflichsten Zwecke der Vorsehung

the binding of a book may be beautiful; but a book can be worth *but* little, if it receives its chief value from the binding der Band eines Buches mag schön seyn; aber ein Buch kann nur wenig Werth haben, wenn es seinen Hauptwerth von dem Einbande empfängt

the knowledge of parts gives often a false view of an object; but the contemplation of the whole leads to truth die Kenntniß einzelner Theile giebt oft eine falsche Ansicht des Gegenstandes; aber die Betrachtung des Ganzen führt zur Wahrheit

act, as much as lies in you, prudently and wisely: what was before you, will also be after you, if it is to be; time will pursue its great course and complete its part handle, so viel an dir ist, klug und weise: was vor dir war, wird auch hinter dir seyn, wenn es seyn soll; ihren großen Gang wird die Zeit gehen, und das Ihrige vollenden

there are certain properties of mind which, like the colour of the skin or the features of the face, may alter, without the whole man *being* affected by it; but there are others with the change of which the man's whole self is altered es giebt gewisse Eigenschaften des Geistes, welche, wie die Farbe des Körpers (or der Haut) und die Züge des Gesichtes, wechseln können, ohne daß dadurch der ganze Mensch affectirt (or affizirt, or berührt) wird; aber es giebt andere, mit deren Abänderung sich zugleich das Selbst des Menschen abändert

the tricks of petty gain degrade the mind, but slavery degrades human nature die Künste des kleinen Gewinns erniedrigen den Geist, Sklaverei aber die menschliche Natur

all violence begins with a show of justice alle Gewaltthätigkeit hebt mit gerechtem Scheine an the moral law is nothing else but the sum of the duties of man living in society die Moral ist nichts anders, als der Inbegriff der Pflichten des in Gesellschaft lebenden Menschen

it cannot be objectionable to read at times and under particular circumstances for pleasure and amusement; but the chief aim can and ought to be no other than the improvement of the mind and heart es kann nicht tadelhaft seyn, zuweilen und unter Umständen zum Vergnügen und Zeitvertreib zu lesen; aber der Hauptzweck kann und darf kein anderer seyn, als die Bildung des Geistes und des Herzens

few have a claim to our heart, but all to our indulgence auf unser Herz haben Wenige, auf unsere Nachsicht Alle Anspruch

the reading of many novels produces a one-sided development of mind, and impairs the taste viele Romane lesen giebt eine einseitige Bildung, und schadet dem guten Geschmack

but too often we satisfy ourselves upon our faults by the thought that others too have faults nur zu oft beruhigen wir uns bei unsern Fehlern damit, daß andere (doch) auch Fehler haben

true happiness is contentment, and that has enough every where das wahre Glück ist die Genügsamkeit, und diese hat überall genug

even the intention to amend may do much for us schon mit dem Vorsatz sich zu bessern, kann es der Mensch weit bringen

when the lion hunts with the fox, he is ashamed of the fox, but not of the cunning der Löwe schämt sich, wenn er mit dem Fuchs jagt, des Fuchses, nicht der List

every thing that refers to language, art, and science, is and must be raised above national antipathies; for this is not the property of the citizen, but of man, — a common possession of the world Alles, was Sprache, Kunst und Wissenschaft umschließt, ist und muß über den Nationalhaß erhaben seyn; denn dies ist kein Eigenthum des Bürgers, sondern des Menschen,—ein Gemeingut der Erde

affectation prevents people from *being* what they are, and yet does not allow them to be what they are not die Affectation verhindert zu seyn, was man ist, und erlaubt doch nicht zu seyn, was man nicht ist

most great things have been accomplished by small nations or by men of little power but great minds die meisten großen Dinge sind durch kleine Völker oder Männer von geringer Macht aber großem Geiste vollbracht worden

our most lawful and most charitable actions lose all worth, if they spring from selfishness unsere gesetzmäßigsten und wohlthätigsten Handlungen verlieren alles Verdienst, wenn der Eigennutz ihre Quelle ist

if I know not, *how* the Supreme Being acts, I know that he does act—my eyes convince me of it weiß ich nicht, wie das höchste Wesen wirkt, so weiß ich doch, daß es wirkt—meine Augen überzeugen mich davon

he who will not be content with little, will not be satisfied with wealth wem nicht an wenig genügt, den macht kein Reichthum satt

the soul of conversation in France is wit, in England, thought in Frankreich ist Witz, in England der Gedanke die Seele des Umgangs,

he who trembles for nothing, loves nothing wer für nichts zittert, liebt auch nichts

order has more influence on the sentiments and the life of men than is commonly believed Ordnung hat einen größern Einfluß auf die Gesinnungen und das Leben der Menschen, als man oft vermeint

he who does not believe in virtue is without it himself wer nicht an Tugend glaubt, hat selber keine

we are not born *with* but *for* virtue wir werden nicht mit der Tugend, sondern zur Tugend geboren

nature requires much less than we imagine die Natur bedarf weit minder, als wir glauben

love of man, if it were possible, would be truly more than love of country and love of our fellow-citizens Menschenliebe, wenn sie seyn könnte, wäre wahrlich mehr als Vaterlands- und Bürgerliebe

what one does not fear to lose, one has never believed to possess and never desired was man nicht zu verlieren fürchtet, hat man nie zu besitzen geglaubt und nie gewünscht

he who has devoted himself to the service of truth, must also

MISCELLANEOUS SENTENCES.

ot shrink for the sake of truth, f need be, to be misunderstood, annoyed and hated — wer sich dem Dienste der Wahrheit geweiht hat, der muß sich auch nicht weigern, um der Wahrheit willen, wenn es seyn muß, verkannt, geneckt und angefeindet zu werden

education begins at school, is extended at college, and is carried on with the majority of mankind in maturer age in the churches — von den Schulen geht die Bildung aus, auf der Universität wird sie erweitert, und in den Kirchen wird der größte Theil der Menschen im reifern Alter fortgebildet

as in different parts of the globe the needle varies in its declension, although under the same leading laws, so the imagination, taste, and manner of writing of nations vary, and it is still and remains every where the same human nature — wie an verschiedenen Orten der Erde die Magnetnadel verschieden jedoch unter Hauptgesetzen declinirt (or abweicht), so declinirt (or weicht) die Einbildungskraft, der Geschmack, die Art der Composition der Völker (ab), und es ist und bleibt doch allenthalben dieselbe Menschheit

among the class of men called scholars some are merely destined to transmit the truths already known and to teach knowledge; others, to expand it; the third, to apply it to life and the real use of society — unter der Klasse von Menschen, die man Gelehrte nennt, sind einige bloß dazu bestimmt, die schon bekannten Wahrheiten fortzupflanzen, und die Wissenschaft zu dociren (or lehren); andere zu erweitern; die dritten, sie auf das menschliche Leben und den wirklichen Nutzen der Gesellschaft anzuwenden

in many cases an inclination to solitude is almost the same to the soul as inclination to sleep is to the weary body — in vielen Fällen ist Neigung zur Einsamkeit für die Seele, was Neigung zum Schlafe für den müden Leib ist

prejudice and superstition only produce evil — Vorurtheil und Aberglaube können nur Böses stiften anger wishes the human race (to have) but one neck, love one heart, and pride two bended knees der Zorn wünscht dem Menschengeschlechte nur einen einzigen Hals, die Liebe ein einziges Herz, und der Stolz zwei gebogene Knie

one person delights in solitude, because he likes to rest undisturbed, and the other, because he likes to work undisturbed der eine liebt die Einsamkeit, weil er gern ungestört ruht, und der andere, weil er gern ungestört arbeitet

every virtue, every prejudice has its home, wherever men dwell jede Tugend, jedes Vorurtheil hat ein Vaterland, so weit Menschen wohnen

every thing has two sides: the chief thing is that we should know and choose the best ein jedes Ding hat zwei Seiten: die Hauptsache ist, daß man die beste kenne und wähle

whoever wishes to improve himself through reading must neither read too much nor fast wem es (darum) zu thun ist, sich durch Lesen zu bilden, darf weder zu viel noch schnell lesen

each season offers us something peculiar; in each we have to do something different; each teaches and encourages; each calls up new wants and wishes jede Jahreszeit giebt uns etwas Eigenes; in jeder muß man etwas anderes verrichten; jede lehrt und muntert auf; in jeder erwachsen neue Bedürfnisse und Wünsche

to the night of sleep follows the morning of waking auf die Nacht des Schlafes folgt der Morgen des Erwachens

a book is a letter which one writes to all unknown friends one has in the world ein Buch ist ein Brief, den man an alle unbekannte Freunde schreibt, die man in der Welt hat

the senses hurry on the understanding to many rash judgments die Sinne verleiten den Verstand zu mancher Uebereilung im Urtheilen

it is on the paths of wisdom that man goes to fame, not on those of pleasure auf den Pfaden der Weisheit wandelt der Mensch zum Ruhme, nicht auf denen des Vergnügens

M

that which we are and which we have to be in the world do not always go together was man ist, und was man in der Welt seyn muß, paßt nicht immer

satiety leads many to separate from the world Sattheit führet sehr viele Menschen zur Absonderung von der Welt

---

IDIOMATIC PHRASES.

to leave in the lurch im Stiche lassen

it does not lie with me es liegt nicht an mir

I do not care for it es liegt mir nichts daran

she was much concerned for (interested in) it es war ihr viel daran gelegen

what is the matter with you? was haben Sie?

what do I care for it? was geht es mich an?

it does not signify es hat nichts zu sagen

he works hard er läßt es sich sauer werden

who can help it? wer kann dafür?

I could not help it ich konnte nichts dafür

now, he is puzzled jetzt stehen die Ochsen am Berge

now, out with it! don't keep it in the back-ground nun, heraus damit! halten Sie nicht damit hinter dem Berge

he always blunders on (speaks without consideration) er fällt immer mit der Thüre in's Haus

according to circumstances nach der Beschaffenheit der Umstände

he was sent off with a flea in his ear er mußte mit langer Nase abziehen

the thing will not succeed die Sache kommt zu nichts

the young people are quite degenerated die jungen Leute sind ganz aus der Art geschlagen

without any farther to do mir nichts, dir nichts

to do a thing unprepared (without much trouble) etwas von der Hand schlagen

IDIOMATIC PHRASES.

he has neither house nor home
er hat weder Dach noch Fach

he has yielded to his fate with a
good grace er hat sich mit Un-
stand in sein Schicksal gefunden

large as the house is, I shall know
how to find my way in it so
groß das Haus ist, werde ich mich
doch darin zu finden wissen

I shall find the rest of the way
easily enough ich werde mich auf
dem übrigen Weg leicht zurecht
finden

just assist her a little, if she wants
it gehen Sie ihr doch ein wenig
an die Hand, wenn Sie es bedarf

you surely won't be led to believe
such nonsense! Sie werden sich
doch nicht solch unsinniges Zeug
aufbürden (or weiß machen) lassen!

we shall see das findet sich

you might interpose with advantage Sie könnten sich mit Vortheil in's Mittel schlagen

the medicine took no effect das
Mittel schlug nicht an

I hope it will turn out to your
advantage ich hoffe, es werde zu
Ihrem Vortheil ausschlagen

the fright has quite paralised me
der Schreck ist mir ganz in die
Glieder geschlagen

that is all the same to me das
gilt mir alles gleich

he was quite indifferent to the
offer er war ganz gleichgültig
gegen das Anerbieten

his indifference really offended
me ich fand seine Gleichgültigkeit
wirklich beleidigend

what you said, was intended for
me was Sie sagten, galt mit

what is the wager? was gilt die
Wette?

what is the price of a bushel of
wheat at Dantsic? was gilt der
Scheffel Weizen zu Danzig?

my happiness is at stake es gilt
mein Glück

one cannot please you in any
thing man kann Ihnen nichts
recht machen

I am determined once for all to
ease my mind, and he shall
answer me ich bin entschlossen,
meinem Herzen ein für alle Mal
Luft zu machen, und er soll mir
Rede stehen

that is just like you das heißt Sy-
nen ähnlich

I cannot make head or tail of him
ich kann nicht aus ihm klug werden

163

IDIOMATIC PHRASES.

I do not know what to think of
Ferdinand ist mit ihr
she had much influence at court
sie galt viel bei Hofe

this coin is not current with us
diese Münze gilt nicht bei uns

every thing is becoming in the
rich and noble den Reichen und
Vornehmen steht alles wohl an

can you not rid me of this troublesome fellow? können Sie mir
diesen unangenehmen Kerl nicht
vom Halse schaffen?

when he is here, I always feel
inclined to yawn wenn er hier
ist, kömmt mir immer das Gäh-
nen an

we will let the matter rest here
wir wollen die Sache hier beruhen lassen

if you can put up with a plain
dinner, you are welcome wenn
Sie mit einem einfachen Essen
fürlieb nehmen können, so sollen
Sie mir willkommen seyn

how do you think to make up for
it? wie denken Sie es wieder gut
zu machen?

such a thing may occasionally
happen, so etwas (or dergleichen)
trifft sich wohl

be it so! immerhin!

I don't care for his anger ich frage
nichts nach seinem Zorn

that is still the question das frägt
sich noch

they are very proud of their noble
extraction sie thun was sich auf
ihre adelige Herkunft zu Gute

I don't care for it ich mache mir
nichts daraus

he has always been disgusting to
my sight er ist mir allezeit ein
Dorn im Auge gewesen

I could never please them ich
konnte ihnen nie etwas Recht
machen

she got out of the frying-pan-into
the fire sie gerieth aus dem Regen in die Traufe

you may indeed boast, it is of no
use Sie haben sich gut brüsten,
es hilft zu nichts

I will not be made a fool of by
you ich werde mich von Ihnen
nicht bei der Nase herumführen
lassen

for the present I do not know
how to bring it about dar der
Hand weiß ich nicht, wie ich es
dahin bringen soll.

J. Wertheimer & Co. Printers, Circus Place, Finsbury Circus.

Printed in the United States
116838LV00005B/150/A